MISSION:

Accepted!

U.S. College Admissions

for

International Students

CHRISTINE HEES

All rights reserved, including the right to reproduce this book or portions thereof in any form whatsoever. The author has made every effort to provide accurate information and internet addresses at the time of publication but does not assume responsibility for errors or changes that may have occurred after publication. Further, the author does not have any control over, nor assume responsibility for, third-party websites or their content.

Copyright © 2024 Christine Hees

ISBN: 979-8-218-44000-8

Publisher: Periwinkle Tide Publishing

Library of Congress Control Number: 2024911490

www.missionaccepted.international

For L.S., N.B., and E.P.

CONTENTS

INTRODUCTION	11
CHAPTER 1 – THE EARLY YEARS	1
ELEMENTARY SCHOOL	3
MIDDLE OR JUNIOR HIGH SCHOOL	4
CHAPTER 2 – HIGH SCHOOL	6
GRADUATION REQUIREMENTS	8
GRADING SYSTEM	9
ADVANCED PLACEMENT COURSES	12
CLASS RANK	16
ANOTHER LOOK AT MATH	17
THE TRANSCRIPT	21
THE SCHOOL PROFILE	22
INTERNATIONAL BACCALAUREATE PROGRAM	23
CHAPTER 3 – STANDARDIZED TESTING	25
THE SAT	26
THE PSAT SUITE	28
THE ACT	29
RECENT TRENDS IN STANDARDIZED TESTING	30
TEST PREP: BIG BUSINESS	32
WHY ALL THIS TESTING?	33
CHAPTER 4 – THE AMERICAN COLLEGE LANDSCAPE	37
TYPES OF COLLEGES	37
THE IVY LEAGUE	43
U.S. COLLEGE RANKINGS	51
U.S. DEGREES	53
CHAPTER 5 – CALIFORNIA'S THREE-TIER MODEL	59
CALIFORNIA COMMUNITY COLLEGES	59
THE CALIFORNIA STATE UNIVERSITY	62
THE UNIVERSITY OF CALIFORNIA	65
CHAPTER 6 – THE ADMISSIONS PROCESS	78

THE ADMISSIONS OFFICE	78
HOW DOES THE EVALUATION PROCESS WORK?	80
HOLISTIC REVIEW BEYOND ACADEMICS	83
ADMISSION PLANS	86
APPLICATION PLATFORMS	97
POSSIBLE APPLICATION OUTCOMES	103

CHAPTER 7 – QUALITATIVE COMPONENTS OF AN APPLICATION — 113

PERSONAL INFORMATION	115
COLLEGE ESSAYS	116
LETTERS OF RECOMMENDATION	120
EXTRACURRICULAR ACTIVITIES AND AWARDS	123
INTERVIEWS	127
VIDEOS	130
SUPPLEMENTAL MATERIALS	131
INTERNATIONAL SPECIFICS	134

CHAPTER 8 – ADMISSIONS CONSIDERATIONS BEYOND ACADEMICS — 137

INSTITUTIONAL PRIORITIES	138
EVALUATING APPLICANTS WITHIN THEIR LOCAL CONTEXT	153

CHAPTER 9 – IMPROVING YOUR PROFILE — 156

ACADEMIC RIGOR: DEPTH AND BREADTH	156
REASONS NOT TO REJECT YOU	161
REASONS TO ADMIT YOU	165

CHAPTER 10 – TIPS FOR WRITING YOUR ESSAYS — 175

GENERAL WRITING STRATEGIES	175
THE PERSONAL STATEMENT	179
THE PERSONAL INTEREST QUESTIONS	182
THE 'WHY US?' ESSAY	184

CHAPTER 11 – APPLICATION STRATEGIES — 186

STEP 1: IDENTIFY YOUR NEEDS AND WANTS	186
STEP 2: EXPLORE YOUR OPTIONS	188
STEP 3: BUILD A BALANCED SHORTLIST	191
STEP 4: CHECK FOR AFFORDABILITY	194
ADDITIONAL TACTICS	198

CHAPTER 12 – PAYING FOR COLLEGE — 216

COST OF ATTENDANCE	216
FINANCING YOUR COLLEGE EXPERIENCE	219
NEGOTIATING YOUR FINANCIAL AID AWARD	240
MAKING A RATIONAL DECISION	241

CHAPTER 13 – THE VISA PROCESS — 244

OVERVIEW OF THE VISA PROCESS	244
REQUIRED FORMS	247
PREPARING FOR YOUR VISA INTERVIEW	250
MAINTAINING YOUR F-1 STATUS	255

CHECKLISTS — 257

FURTHER READING — 263

ABOUT THE AUTHOR — 265

REFERENCES — 267

x

Introduction

When I attended my first college admissions info night – it must have been in 2017 when my oldest was in 8th grade – I felt like I was teleported to Mars, and the presenter spoke some form of Martian dialect. 'AP, ED, yield protection, A-G, demonstrated interest, LoCI, EA, GPA!'

I left the meeting overwhelmed by all the acronyms and new information thrown at me. As an immigrant who had not attended school or college in the U.S.A., I found this process alien and very different from what I knew. In Germany, students graduate high school with the best 'Abitur' diploma they can achieve and, with a few exceptions, enroll in the university of their choice. Done.

While I walked away from that info night quite confused, I realized two things. First, the college admissions process in America is complex. Second, having good grades may not be enough to be admitted to the college of your dreams. Only later did I learn that it is not about getting into your 'dream school' but finding the college that is the best fit for your unique situation. But I am getting ahead of myself.

After that meeting, I did what I always do when I set my mind to something: I dove head-first into the topic and began my research. I read books and articles, attended campus tours and college information meetings, talked to admissions officers, and combed the Internet for every statistic I could find. In a world where knowledge is power, I educated myself the best I could. By no means do I consider myself an expert, but at some point, I realized that what I had learned about the college admissions process may be helpful to others.

While I wrote this handbook with international students in mind, it may be just as useful for anyone unfamiliar with today's college admissions process: Immigrants like me who want to support and guide their children on their journey to college. Parents who did not have the opportunity to attend college. Students who have their heart set on studying in the U.S.A. Anyone who believes in the transformative power of knowledge.

This handbook encapsulates the essential elements of college admissions that I wish I had known right from the start. But don't take my word for it. Do your own research. Check the deadlines. Dig into the Internet; there is so much information out there.

This book is just the beginning.

Chapter 1 – The Early Years

Before we explore the complexities of American colleges and explore the maze of their admissions process, let us step back and gain a basic understanding of primary and secondary education in the United States. This knowledge will provide context and help us better understand the specific requirements of college admissions. While it is a legal obligation for parents to educate their child, they can choose the type of schooling they prefer. Options range from homeschooling to public and expensive private schools. An estimated 100,000 public and 30,000 private schools educate about 50 million American students in grades K through 12[1].

Public schools, which educate most American students (88%), are funded by the government and local property taxes, making them accessible free of charge. Approximately 9% of students attend private schools, financed through tuition payments. Religious organizations may subsidize parochial schools, allowing them to offer lower tuition rates. The remaining 3% of parents opt for homeschooling, a trend that slightly increased since the COVID-19 pandemic.

Public schools are funded by the government and local property taxes

Private schools often specialize in a particular area such as religious affiliation, advanced academics, language immersion, progressive teaching concepts, or other educational elements. The academic performance standards at public schools vary greatly between the fifty states, with Massachusetts, Connecticut, and New Jersey consistently leading the national rankings[2]. To learn more about a specific school, refer to websites like *greatschools.org*, which ranks American K-12 schools based on academic performance and educational criteria.

The American education system is structured into three distinct sections: elementary, middle, and high school. At the age of five, children enter the educational system in the kindergarten class, where they learn fundamental skills, such as reading and writing. Some school districts offer transitional kindergarten classes for children who missed the official cutoff dates for kindergarten. Additionally, private preschools are available as optional early learning opportunities for children between the ages of two and four.

The American School System

HOMESCHOOLING

Grade 12 (Senior)	
Grade 11 (Junior)	**High**
Grade 10 (Sophomore)	**School**
Grade 9 (Freshman)	

Grade 8	
Grade 7	**Middle**
Grade 6	**School**

Grade 5	
Grade 4	
Grade 3	**Elementary**
Grade 2	**School**
Grade 1	
Kindergarten	

Pre-School
(private/optional)

Chapter 1 – The Early Years

Elementary School

The American educational system begins with elementary schools, which instruct children from kindergarten through the fifth or sixth grade. During these years, homeroom teachers teach the primary subjects of English Language Arts, math, social studies, and science. Depending on funding and resources, some schools may also offer instruction in physical education, music, and arts. Elementary school curricula are guided by state-mandated academic standards that outline the expected learning objectives and proficiency levels for each grade.

Throughout elementary school, students remain in the same homeroom for the entire academic year, with classes being mixed annually. The average class size in elementary schools ranges from 20 to 30 students. The teaching approach emphasizes interactive and student-centered learning, encouraging collaboration, communication, and problem-solving skills through group activities and classroom discussions.

> Elementary schools cover kindergarten through 5th or 6th grades

Assessments are crucial in tracking student progress and involve teacher evaluations, project-based assessments, and standardized tests. However, there is an ongoing debate surrounding the necessity, frequency, and impact of standardized testing on elementary students. Most elementary schools recognize the role parents play in their child's education and encourage them to actively participate through parent-teacher conferences, volunteering opportunities, and school events.

Middle or Junior High School

The transition from childhood to adolescence occurs between eleven and fourteen years. During this time of major developmental changes, students enter middle school as children and leave as adolescents. Middle school or junior high school serves as a bridge between elementary and high school education. It typically encompasses grades six through eight, but some school districts may include only grades seven and eight. Several elementary schools feed into one middle school, leading to a significantly larger student population.

> Middle school (6th through 8th grades) prepares for the high school system

A fundamental change in middle school is the shift from a single-classroom environment to a departmentalized model with subject-specific teachers. Students rotate through different classrooms each period, encountering new peers in each class. This approach mimics the high school model and fosters time management and independence as students navigate between six and seven courses daily. Electives, such as foreign languages, arts, technology, and music, supplement the core academics of English, math, science, and social studies.

In mathematics, some middle schools implement a practice known as 'math tracking,' which groups students based on their mathematical abilities. A placement test typically determines the appropriate track, ranging from remedial to advanced math. Proponents argue that this approach allows for more targeted and challenging instruction for advanced

> Math tracking may place advanced middle school students in a high school math class

Chapter 1 – The Early Years

students while providing additional support for those who need it. Critics of math tracking, however, express concerns about potential inequalities and the long-term impact on academic outcomes.

In highly competitive school districts, such as the Palo Alto Unified School District[3] in the heart of Silicon Valley, many families hire private tutors to gain a competitive edge in their child's academic performance. These professional tutors help with homework and teach a deeper understanding of mathematical concepts. They also prepare their students for math placement tests, increasing their chances of being tracked into the most advanced class available. Placement in the higher math track gives students a head-start for high school, as they often take courses, such as algebra or geometry, in middle school instead of high school.

> Some families hire private tutors to maximize their child's performance

However, the ability to afford expensive supplemental tutoring services highlights a potential advantage for students from affluent families over their less privileged peers from a young age. This discrepancy fuels ongoing debates about the fairness and potential long-term consequences of allowing some students to accelerate their academics beyond the traditional middle school curriculum.

Chapter 2 – High School

After completing eighth grade, American students transition once again, this time entering high school, which encompasses grades nine through twelve. Many Hollywood movies dramatize the social dynamics in American high schools. Still, films like *Mean Girls* or *Clueless* do not give a realistic account of the academic environment and overall student experience.

American high schools are inclusive environments, catering to a diverse student population with varying abilities, needs, and aspirations. They serve the most academically gifted, average students, and those requiring special educational support. This diversity calls for multiple distinct academic pathways to facilitate each student. Individualized Education Programs and 504 Plans provide specialized educational services and accommodations for students with disabilities and learning differences. Additionally, high schools offer vocational and technical education options, equipping students with practical life skills applicable to various careers.

> American high schools are inclusive and teach a diverse student body

Chapter 2 – High School

The high school curriculum prepares students for higher education or entry into the workforce. Students can select their courses from an extensive list of offerings based on their interests and goals. Typically, American students take six subjects each year, including the core areas such as English, mathematics, sciences, foreign languages, and social studies. They may add an optional seventh subject as an elective. In a traditional schedule, each subject is taught every day. Some high schools, however, adopt a block schedule, where students have fewer classes per day, but each class period is longer. Instead of having six or seven shorter classes, students might have only three or four classes, each lasting from 60 to 90 minutes. Block schedules can vary, with some schools using an alternating day format where students have different courses on different days. Others may have a fixed schedule with certain classes meeting on specific days of the week.

> American students take up to six or seven subjects per year

High schools, particularly large and well-funded ones, offer various course options, ranging from academic subjects like calculus to non-academic electives such as woodworking, digital media design, and drama. This variety enables students to explore various interests and specialize in areas that align with their talents and career goals.

> High schools offer academic and non-academic subjects

Many schools utilize online platforms where students can monitor their academic progress for each class in real time. Grades are transparent and reflect the performance in individual assignments such as tests, exams, projects, and graded homework.

Extracurricular activities are an integral part of the American high school experience. Participation in sports teams, clubs, arts programs, or community service contribute to the well-rounded student profile that colleges seek in applicants. Active participation in extracurricular activities can showcase a student's leadership abilities and commitment to challenge themselves beyond academics.

> Students can monitor their academic performance online

Graduation Requirements

Graduation requirements vary from state to state, across school districts, and between public and private high schools. Each state and district establishes the minimum requirements students must fulfill to earn a high school diploma. For instance, the State of California[4] mandates that high school students complete at least the following coursework to graduate:

English:	3 years
Math (including Algebra 1):	2 years
Science (biological and physical):	2 years
Social studies:	3 years
Arts, world language, career technical education:	1 year
Physical education:	2 years
Ethnic Studies (starting 2026):	0.5 years

However, these state-mandated minimum graduation requirements do not necessarily align with the admissions criteria set by various colleges. Each college has its own set of requirements for prospective applicants, which may exceed or differ from the state's minimum standards for high school graduation. This means that the minimum graduation requirements for a state or high school may not be sufficient to apply to a prospective college. Given this complexity, American students typically plan their high school courses well in advance. They must ensure they meet the graduation criteria of their state and school as well as any additional requirements imposed by prospective colleges. This strategic course planning is essential to position themselves competitively in college admissions.

Grading System

Most high schools employ two methods to evaluate academic performance: letter grades and grade point average (GPA). Letter grades are alphabetic representations of a student's performance in a specific course, such as English or World History. These grades typically range from A (excellent) to F (failing), with A, B, C, and D being passing grades. Each letter grade corresponds to a percentage of correct responses or points earned out of the total possible for an assignment, exam, or the entire course. Some schools may use '+' and '-' modifiers to further differentiate performance within a letter grade, for example, A+, A, and A-.

A: 4.0 (90-100%)
B: 3.0 (80-89%)
C: 2.0 (70-79%)
D: 1.0 (60-69%)
F: 0.0 (0-59%)

Occasionally, high schools permit students to take a limited number of courses under a 'pass/no pass' grading scheme. This option allows students to forgo receiving a letter grade for the class. Instead, the student's academic record reflects whether they passed or failed the course. Usually, students can retake a failed class over the summer or during the next school year, but the 'F' will still appear on their transcript.

> GPA = academic performance in grades 9 through 12 in one number

The second system, the GPA or grade point average, is a standardized measure of academic achievement. It condenses a student's performance across all courses taken during grades 9 through 12 into a single cumulative number. This allows for easier comparison between students and provides a uniform, quantitative measure of academic achievement. The GPA is a standard metric for college admissions and in scholarship applications.

Most schools use a GPA scale from 0.0 to 4.0, with 4.0 being the highest achievable GPA. A student's GPA is calculated by assigning numerical values to their letter grades and then averaging them. For example, an 'A' may be equivalent to 4.0, a 'B' to 3.0, etc. While some high schools include physical education or other non-academic subjects like peer tutoring in the student's GPA, others include only academic subjects.

This grading system is further nuanced by adjusting the GPA based on the difficulty of classes, resulting in the weighted GPA. More rigorous courses, such as honors and Advanced Placement, boost a student's weighted GPA. Since American students can take classes with varying

Chapter 2 – High School

levels of academic rigor, their report card or transcript usually indicates both the unweighted and weighted GPAs.

Honors classes, which offer a more rigorous curriculum than standard courses, are weighted more heavily when calculating the weighted GPA. For instance, many high schools assign 4.5 points instead of the standard 4.0 for an 'A' in an honors class. Thus, a student taking an honors English class will end up with a higher weighted GPA than their friend taking the regular English class, assuming they both receive the same letter grade. The weighted GPA encourages students to challenge themselves academically and take more rigorous courses. In addition, if a student starts with lower grades in their freshman year, they can boost their weighted GPA by taking more challenging courses in following years.

> For college admissions, all grades from freshman to senior year count!

From Individual Assignments to GPA

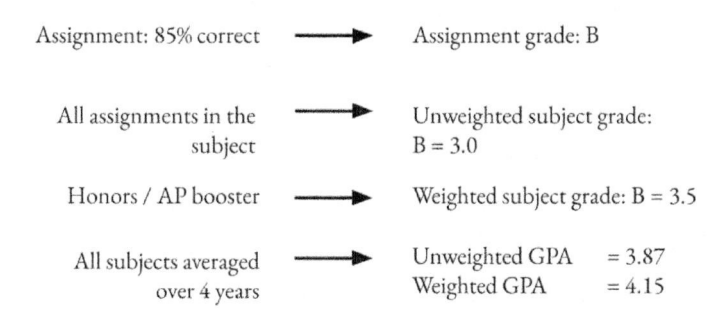

Assignment: 85% correct ⟶ Assignment grade: B

All assignments in the subject ⟶ Unweighted subject grade: B = 3.0

Honors / AP booster ⟶ Weighted subject grade: B = 3.5

All subjects averaged over 4 years ⟶ Unweighted GPA = 3.87
Weighted GPA = 4.15

In summary, the GPA reflects a student's academic performance during grades 9 through 12, condensed into a single number. When weighted, it accounts for the rigor of classes a student has taken. The GPA is derived from all performance assessments across multiple subjects and accumulated over four years, making all four high school years crucial for college admissions!

Advanced Placement Courses

> AP classes are college-level courses ending in a standardized exam

For students eager to challenge themselves even more, many schools offer AP courses, which are college-level classes taught at high schools. These rigorous courses cover a wide range of subjects, from sciences and mathematics to humanities and arts, allowing students to explore various fields in greater depth. At the end of the school year, students can sit for the corresponding AP exam in their chosen subjects. The standardized exams, created and evaluated by the College Board, feature a combination of multiple-choice questions and free-response sections. High schools serve as testing sites, facilitating the administration of these exams on their campus. AP exams are scored on a scale of 1 to 5, with 3, 4, and 5 considered passing scores.

AP exams taken between 9th and 12th grade are valid until a student begins college. The College Board archives exam scores after four years, but students can retrieve them from the archives and send them to colleges[5] if

> On a scale from 1 to 5, passing AP scores are 3, 4, and 5

needed for the application process. While AP scores do not expire, colleges may not accept them for credit if older than four or five years. Students can retake an AP exam, but both scores will be reported to colleges unless explicitly requested to withhold one[6]. Each AP exam costs $98 if taken in the U.S.A. or Canada and $128 for all other countries. Some students may qualify for a fee reduction.

AP classes increase the student's GPA and demonstrate academic rigor

Earning passing scores on the AP exam offers multiple benefits. Some colleges grant course credits for AP exams with a minimum score, usually a three or higher. Getting credits for their AP exams may allow students to bypass introductory or general education courses at college, giving them the time to pursue more advanced courses or allowing them to graduate faster than the traditional four-year timeline. Another significant benefit of the AP program is the preparation it offers for the rigors of college-level work. Students enrolled in AP courses develop essential skills, such as critical thinking, analytical writing, and in-depth study habits. This can ease the transition from high school to college, making students more prepared for the rigors of higher education. Moreover, success in AP exams holds value in the college admissions process, as it demonstrates a student's ability to handle rigorous academic work.

Additionally, AP courses are weighted more heavily in GPA calculations than regular courses, reflecting their increased difficulty and complexity. An 'A' in an AP class could be valued at 5.0 on the 4.0 GPA scale, as opposed to a 4.0 in a regular class,

By taking honors and AP classes, a student's GPA can exceed 4.0

significantly boosting the weighted GPA. Some students take only honors and AP classes in all six or seven subjects, potentially increasing their GPA far beyond the 4.0 scale.

Colleges often assess both, the weighted and unweighted GPAs. Weighted GPAs can provide context about a student's course load, and a GPA over 4.0 indicates great academic performance in more rigorous classes. The unweighted GPA may offer a standard metric for comparison across different high schools. However, to the surprise of many students, colleges may not take their GPA at face value. Many admissions offices use their own algorithm to recalculate a student's GPA. For example, the University of California only considers grades in pre-defined core subjects during applicants' 10th and 11th grades.

> Many colleges recalculate a student's GPA using their own formula

Let us take a fictitious example to illustrate the difference between weighted and unweighted GPAs. In her junior year, Lauren takes six academic subjects and one elective. Four classes are AP courses, two are honors classes, and one is a regular class. Lauren's high school uses a standard formula that boosts each AP class with one additional point and each honors class with an extra 0.5 points.

Typical conversion table for honors (+0.5) and AP classes (+ 1.0):

Letter Grade	Unweighted GPA	Honors Class: Weighted GPA	AP Class: Weighted GPA
A	4.0	4.5	5.0
B	3.0	3.5	4.0
C	2.0	2.5	3.0

Chapter 2 – High School

At the end of her junior year, Lauren's transcript displays her courses, grades, and both her unweighted and weighted GPAs. Her high school calculates the weighted GPA based on the standard conversion table.

Lauren's courses and unweighted grades:

AP English Literature & Composition	A (4.0)
AP Calculus A/B	B (3.0)
AP Biology	A (4.0)
AP United States History	B (3.0)
Honors Spanish II	A (4.0)
Honors Physics	B (3.0)
Drama I (regular class)	A (4.0)

Unweighted GPA:

(4.0 + 3.0 + 4.0 + 3.0 + 4.0 + 3.0 + 4.0) / 7 = 25 / 7 = **3.57**

Weighted GPA:

(5.0 + 4.0 + 5.0 + 4.0 + 4.5 + 3.5 + 4.0) / 7 = 30 / 7 = **4.29**

As her honors and AP classes are boosted with 0.5 and 1.0 points each, Lauren's weighted GPA of 4.29 is significantly higher than her unweighted GPA of 3.57.

This example illustrates that:

→ Taking more rigorous honors and AP classes improves a student's weighted GPA.
→ A student's weighted GPA can exceed 4.0 on a standard 4.0 scale!
→ The conversion formula used by the high school significantly impacts a student's weighted GPA. Lauren's weighted GPA would

be 5.0 if her school boosted AP classes by 2.0 points and honors classes by 1.0 (instead of 1.0 and 0.5 points).
→ Different high schools may use different formulas, making direct comparisons between two applicants difficult.
→ Since there is no standard formula applied by all high schools, colleges often recalculate the GPA using their own algorithm to ensure they can compare all applicants in a consistent manner.

Class Rank

While ranking their students based on academic performance was once a standard practice in American high schools, it has become less common in recent years. Again, variability is the name of the game. For those high schools that still rank their students, the primary purpose is to formally recognize and reward top academic achievers with honors, awards, or distinctions. Class rankings can also play a role in college admissions or the awarding of scholarships.

> Valedictorian = top ranked student(s) in a graduating class

Typically, a student's GPA determines their rank, but some schools also factor in standardized test scores, the difficulty of coursework undertaken, or non-academic electives. In certain instances, high schools may assign the top rank to all students with an unweighted GPA of 4.0, potentially resulting in multiple

> Some high schools provide class rank to admission officers on demand

valedictorians within a single graduating class. Some high schools do not disclose rankings to their students but provide them upon request to a college during the admissions process. Others include a grade distribution table for every graduating class in their school profile. Again, there is a high degree of variability across American high schools.

Class rankings have faced criticism for oversimplifying a student's academic abilities and potential into a single numerical value. Critics argue that this approach fails to capture the full breadth of a student's skills, achievements, and talents. Additionally, there are concerns that ranking systems may foster an unhealthy competitive environment among students, potentially contributing to increased stress levels and hindering the overall learning experience.

In response to these concerns, many high schools have opted moved away from ranking systems. This is particularly true for highly competitive academic schools, which are wary of potential disadvantages their students may face in college admissions. A student could excel academically and still not be among the top-ranked individuals due to the high school's competitive nature.

Another Look at Math

American high schools educate students from all walks of life and with various academic interests. Therefore, they need to offer classes that fit their diverse student population. In the highly competitive educational landscape, many American families start thinking about college admissions when their children are still young. Some parents aim to boost their child's academics through tutoring services in hopes of accelerating their child's academic path. Do you remember that advanced middle school students can already take high school algebra classes? Unlike other subjects, math follows a predefined sequence, as mathematical concepts logically build upon each other. Most high schools offer multiple pathways for math, catering to students with varying levels of aptitude and interest, ranging from basic to college-level concepts. In addition, colleges usually place particular emphasis on the level of math courses applicants have completed. With these considerations in mind, let us examine the multiple math options a high school may provide.

The standard path begins with foundational algebra and geometry courses and usually progresses to calculus. Optional classes include statistics, data science, and multivariate analysis. Usually, each class is taught for one academic year, allowing the students to dive deep into one specific area before focusing on the next one. According to the Common Core standards, a set of minimum academic standards across the United States, the typical order of core high school math from freshman to senior year consists of Algebra 1, Geometry, Algebra 2, Pre-calculus or Trigonometry, and Calculus.

- Pre-algebra
- Algebra 1
- Geometry
- Algebra 2
- Trigonometry or Pre-calculus
- Calculus
- Statistics (opt.)
- Data Science (opt.)
- Multivariate Analysis (opt.)

High schools commonly provide three main tracks: regular, honors, and AP classes. In the regular track, students begin with Algebra 1, continue with precalculus, and may conclude their high school math path with statistics or applied math, which covers essential concepts without the intensity of more advanced tracks. Honors classes, on the other hand, are a good fit for students seeking a more challenging curriculum as they dive deeper into mathematical theory and applications.

The most advanced track is the AP program. These classes offer college-level material and culminate in a standardized exam. Passing the AP exam demonstrates proficiency in advanced math. It may

3 tracks per subject:
Regular, honors, & AP

also lead to college credits, which can accelerate upper-class standing, giving students priority in selecting their college courses and potentially cutting their time to graduation. High school students may have multiple AP options, such as AP calculus and AP statistics. In some schools, multivariable analysis is available through local community colleges.

-AP Pre-calculus
-AP Calculus A/B
-AP Calculus B/C
-AP Statistics

The AP calculus curriculum consists of two distinct courses: Calculus A/B, which covers fundamental concepts of limits, derivatives, and integrals, and Calculus B/C, which extends into more advanced topics like series and parametric equations. AP statistics focuses on the interpretation and analysis of data, exploring statistical concepts and methodologies. Some high schools may offer a course in multivariable analysis, which expands upon the material covered in Calculus B/C. Multivariable analysis introduces students to partial derivatives, multiple integrals, and vector calculus.

In terms of curriculum structure, high schools can adopt a subject-specific or integrated math approach. Typically, the American system utilizes the concept of subject-specific math, dedicating an entire school year to a particular area. For instance, students may take Geometry in one year and Algebra 2 in the following year. This traditional approach allows in-depth exploration of each mathematical topic. More recently, states like North Carolina, Utah, and West Virginia switched to integrated math, a concept used in many European countries.

> Subject-specific math teaches one math topic in a year-long course

Integrated math programs take a different approach by connecting the various mathematical concepts throughout each academic year. Students revisit and build upon multiple areas, integrating algebraic, geometric, and statistical concepts within the same school year. The integrated math model encourages students to see the relationships between different mathematical areas. Both educational approaches have their merits, and the choice is often influenced by state requirements, the school district's preferences, or the high school's educational philosophy.

> Integrated math covers all math topics progressively every year

However, the acceleration of advanced math also comes with downsides. While some students struggle to follow the accelerated math progression, others may run out of high school courses before their senior year. This can be particularly true for students who accelerate through coursework too fast or those in schools with limited advanced math offerings. As high schools and colleges require a minimum number of years of math, a student who accelerates their math curriculum too early in middle school or too fast may run out of math options in high school. This situation could negatively affect college admissions if a student has not completed four consecutive years of math during high school.

This phenomenon highlights the need for high schools to provide flexible pathways for students. Solutions may include partnerships with local community colleges for dual enrollment or expanding the high school course catalog. Another option may be to slow down the current race to math proficiency during secondary education and take college-level classes in college.

> Dual enrollment at a community college can offer an additional pathway

The Transcript

At the end of each academic term, whether it is a quarter, trimester, or semester, students receive their formal report card, usually referred to as a transcript. A transcript is a comprehensive record detailing all the courses, corresponding grades, and the student's cumulative GPA since grade 9.

A high school transcript typically includes:

- → Academic records of all core and elective courses
- → Grades in each course
- → Class rank, if applicable
- → Standardized test scores like the SAT, ACT, or AP exams

- → Attendance records
- → Disciplinary action, such as suspensions
- → Awards and Honors

When a high school sends official transcripts to colleges, they must be sealed. Students usually receive unofficial transcripts, which are used for preliminary reviews or personal records. During college admissions, students self-report their grades, and the high school sends an official transcript as official verification once the student has committed to a particular college. Occasionally, a college may ask a high school counselor to upload official transcripts for further review. For admissions purposes, most colleges consider a student's performance in all four years of high school, while others, like the University of California, only evaluate grades ten and eleven.

The School Profile

As college applicants get evaluated in the context of opportunities available to them, high schools create a document known as the school profile. The school profile provides the essential background information to help contextualize a student's achievements and experiences. In addition, the school profile can also prove valuable when students apply for scholarships or seek to transfer to a different high school. The schools' guidance counselor creates the profile; it may include details about the school's mission and teaching philosophy, grading system and scale, class rank and distribution, AP, IB, and other course offerings, extracurricular activities, sports programs, and student demographics. It may also highlight notable achievements, awards, and honors that the school and its students received.

This information helps admissions officers understand applicants' unique challenges and opportunities. Including local context in admissions decisions facilitates a fair and informed evaluation of all applicants. For example, a student

> The school profile provides context, such as available courses or grading policies

who has not taken any AP classes during their four years in high school may be viewed differently depending on the type of opportunities available to them. If a small, rural high school offers no AP courses, colleges will not penalize the student for the lack of opportunities at their school. However, suppose another student attends a well-funded high school in Silicon Valley that offers twenty AP courses. In this case, admissions officers may come to a different conclusion when the student has not taken any challenging coursework. Whatever a student's unique situation, the school profile provides the necessary context to assess them fairly.

International Baccalaureate Program

The International Baccalaureate program is known for its emphasis on international-mindedness, critical thinking, and holistic education. While some American schools follow the IB curriculum for early and middle childhood education, over 900 high schools across the United States offer the IB Diploma Program. Worldwide, the IB Program includes over 5,700 schools in 160 countries[7].

Its global recognition and rigorous reputation benefit students pursuing an IB Diploma, including international students. Earning an IB Diploma can even increase the odds of getting into a highly selective college: Research reveals that admission rates for IB students at Ivy League and other elite colleges are 18% to 22% higher than for non-IB students[8].

> The IB is globally recognized and may provide advantages in college admissions

The IB Diploma Program[9] covers grades eleven and twelve, with students choosing six academic subjects plus the mandatory 'Diploma Program Core.' Students study three of the six subjects at a higher level and three at a standard level. As part of the Diploma Program Core, IB students write an in-depth 4,000-word research paper, the Extended Essay. At the end of 12th grade, the IB program concludes with a final centralized exam. Students receive scores between 1 to 7 points for each academic subject and up to 3 more for the 'Core' components, for a total maximum of 45 points. While colleges know that the IB program does not use GPA, online calculators help students translate their IB scores into GPA[10].

> Colleges may award credits for IB classes with a minimum score

Universities and colleges worldwide recognize the IB Diploma and many award credits for a student's performance in the central IB exams. For example, when students score 30 points or higher on their IB exams, the University of California[11] and Boston University[12] award up to 30 credits toward their college courses.

Chapter 3 – Standardized Testing

Until the pandemic, standardized tests were a cornerstone of college applications and a rite of passage for American teenagers. Almost all admissions offices used them to assess applicants' college readiness. The standardized nature of these tests, with consistent content, format, and scoring, provided a benchmark that allowed to compare all applicants on the same metric.

> Standardized tests assess college readiness and provide a common benchmark

Despite being designed to assess the skills and knowledge necessary for college, standardized tests have recently come under scrutiny. Critics argue these tests can be biased and may not fully capture a student's abilities or potential. This debate was further fueled during the pandemic when most colleges switched to test-optional policies.

However, beginning in 2024, several flagship institutions announced their return to standardized testing policies, suggesting a possible comeback. This chapter examines the specifics of the two most common standardized tests, the SAT and ACT, and the debates surrounding them.

The SAT

The Scholastic Assessment Test[13] was initially modeled after Army IQ tests and was first introduced by the College Board in 1926. It became a standard requirement for applicants to Ivy League colleges in the 1940s. Over the years, the SAT has undergone multiple revisions, with a major overhaul in 2005 that added a written essay and changed the content to better align with high school curricula. In 2016, the SAT returned to the original 1600-point scale and removed penalties for wrong answers.

> The English section tests reading comprehension and grammar skills with an optional essay

Today, the SAT contains two main sections, English and math, with an optional essay required by some colleges. The Evidence-Based Reading and Writing section tests students' reading comprehension and grammar skills. It includes passages from literature, historical documents, social sciences, and scientific articles and requires students to interpret, analyze, and make inferences. The optional essay evaluates the ability to analyze and write coherent arguments. Beginning with August 2024, the SAT registration fee is $68.

The math section covers algebra, geometry, and basic trigonometry, and the questions apply mathematical concepts to real-world scenarios. The SAT score ranges from 400 to 1600, combining the scores from the English and math segments, with each section accounting for a maximum score of 800. Students can take

> English: 200-800
> Math: 200-800
> **Total:** 400-1600

Chapter 3 – Standardized Testing

the SAT multiple times and often use professional preparatory classes to achieve higher scores.

The College Board transitioned the paper-based SAT to a digital format in March 2024. This shift is not just a change in format but a significant step toward modernizing the exam and making it more relevant and accessible. With a total time of about two hours, the digital SAT is about one hour shorter than the paper-based version, offering a more streamlined testing experience.

> Performance in part one determines the level of difficulty of questions in part two

The digital format uses an adaptive approach that adjusts the difficulty of questions based on the test taker's performance in earlier sections. This means that students who perform well in the initial part will be presented with more challenging questions in the second part, giving them the chance to reach the top score. Conversely, a student performing worse in part one will face less difficult questions in the second one; they may still attain a high score but cannot achieve the maximum score of 800.

The digital SAT can be administered more frequently and at more locations, making it easier for students to schedule it at a testing center or their high school. Scores can also be processed and returned to students within days instead of weeks for the paper-based test. Test takers may use a pre-approved calculator or the new in-app graphing calculator. There is no longer a calculator-free math section. The digital format may require students to prepare differently for the SAT. To familiarize yourself with the new

> The SAT now provides a built-in calculator

digital format, download the College Board's Bluebook App[14], which allows you to take four free practice tests.

The PSAT Suite

The College Board offers more standardized tests in addition to the SAT. Until recently, students could take an SAT Subject Test to demonstrate their expertise in a particular subject, such as math, science, English, history, and foreign languages. While they were once a standard component of college applications, the College Board announced their termination in 2021, citing a desire to reduce the demands on students.

> PSAT/NMSQT = Practice for the SAT and qualifies for National Merit Scholarship

On the other hand, the Preliminary SAT suite continues to play a role. It consists of three exams designed to aid younger students in preparing for the SAT. By taking a PSAT test, students familiarize themselves with the format and types of questions they will encounter on the SAT. This can identify areas for improvement and boost their performance in the SAT.

For eighth and ninth graders, the PSAT 8/9 test offers early insights into their academic strengths and areas for improvement; the PSAT 10 serves a similar purpose for tenth graders. Most students take the PSAT/NMSQT in their junior year. While PSAT scores are not considered in college admissions, they provide valuable feedback for future test preparation. Moreover, the PSAT serves as a qualifier for the National Merit Scholarship Program. Each year, the top scorers on the PSAT/NMSQT are designated National Merit Semifinalists, with the potential to advance to 'Finalist' and 'Scholar.' Earning such a scholarship reflects a student's dedication to academic success, may open doors to colleges, and help cover college expenses through scholarships.

The ACT

The American College Testing[15] was introduced in 1959 as a competitor to the SAT. Developed by an education professor at the University of Iowa, the ACT evaluates the educational development of high school students and their ability to complete college-level work. The ACT differs from the SAT in structure and content, focusing more on curriculum-based achievement. It initially included four sections: English, mathematics, social studies, and natural sciences. The social studies section was later replaced by reading, and a writing test was added in 2005. Over time, the ACT gained popularity, especially in the Midwest and Southern states.

Today, the ACT is as widely accepted as the SAT and comprises four mandatory sections: English, mathematics, reading, and science, plus an optional writing test. The English section focuses on grammar, punctuation, sentence structure, and rhetorical skills, while the math section covers pre-algebra, algebra, geometry, and trigonometry. The reading section uses passages from various genres to evaluate reading comprehension, and the science part assesses interpretation, analysis, evaluation, and problem-solving skills in the natural sciences. Like in the SAT, the optional writing section requires the student to write an essay that

English:	1-36
Math:	1-36
Reading:	1-36
Science:	1-36
Total:	**1-36**

presents and supports a perspective on a given issue. ACT scores range from 1 to 36, with the composite score being the average of the four section scores. The fee for the ACT without the essay is $68, and $93 including the essay when taken in the United States. International fees are $181.50 without and $206.50 with the essay.

Recent Trends in Standardized Testing

There have been significant changes in how colleges handle standardized testing. Recent studies indicate a potential correlation between standardized test results and socioeconomic status. Students from more privileged backgrounds consistently achieve higher test scores since they can afford test preparation centers and private tutors. Highlighting this potential bias in standardized tests, experts emphasize the importance of an assessment that includes qualitative aspects beyond academics and test scores. Under this holistic approach, colleges consider a student's overall profile, including their academic achievements, extracurricular activities, personal essays, and letters of recommendation, rather than just their test scores. When the COVID-19 pandemic made it impossible to take tests due to logistical challenges and health concerns, many colleges switched to test-optional policies.

> Test scores may not fully predict a student's academic success in college

With test-optional policies, students decide whether their standardized test scores accurately represent their academic abilities and potential. They can either submit or omit their SAT or ACT scores in their application. Not submitting scores does not impact their application negatively. However, submitted scores will be considered during the evaluation. This approach recognizes that standardized test scores may not always be the most accurate indicators of success, especially for those students lacking access to test preparation resources. Qualitative aspects, such as essays and extracurricular activities, in addition to academics, can offer a more thorough understanding of an applicant. Some colleges, like the University of California, have taken a progressive step further by implementing a test-blind policy. Under this policy, the UCs do not consider standardized tests and have even removed the option to enter scores in their applications. Other colleges have adopted a test-flexible approach, requiring alternative assessment options, such as AP or IB exams, to the SAT and ACT.

Mandatory: SAT or ACT required, e.g. MIT

Test-flexible: SAT, ACT, AP, or IB scores required, e.g. Yale

Test-optional: SAT or ACT considered if submitted, e.g. Johns Hopkins University

Test-blind: Scores not considered, e.g. UC, CSU

The test-optional trend marks a new understanding of assessing college readiness. However, given the variety of implemented policies, it is critical to research all prospective colleges, as their policies may vary or change over time. Some, like the Massachusetts Institute of Technology[16], have already returned to mandatory reporting of test scores in their application. In February 2024, Yale unveiled its test-flexible policy for 2025, requiring applicants to submit either SAT,

ACT, AP, or IB tests. Shortly after, two additional Ivies, Harvard and Brown, reinstated standardized test mandates for fall 2024. These changes indicate a potential return to mandatory testing and underline the importance of staying up to date on current testing policies.

Test Prep: Big Business

Like many things in the United States, college applications and standardized test preparation have become big business opportunities. Forbes Magazine estimates that the U.S. college prep and tutoring market will be worth $8.37 billion by 2025[17]. As students aim to boost their profiles for college admissions, a new industry has developed to help them improve their test scores and odds of admission. This industry spans services like college counseling, subject tutoring, test preparation, and online resources. Companies like Kaplan Test Prep[18] and The Princeton Review[19] provide traditional in-person preparation courses, including practice tests, comprehensive course material, and personalized tutoring. These services can be costly, but they offer the advantage of face-to-face interaction, repeated practice tests, and tailored guidance in small groups or one-on-one.

> The U.S. test prep and tutoring industry is worth over $8 billion

> Khan Academy offers free SAT and AP test preparation

Virtual test prep has recently gained immense popularity as online platforms offer flexible and affordable alternatives by offering video lessons, interactive modules, and practice tests. Khan Academy[20], in partnership with the College Board, offers free, comprehensive online

SAT preparation courses. Online platforms not only provide convenience and adaptability but also cater to a broad range of learning styles with customizable study plans and on-demand resources. This democratization of resources is an important step toward leveling the playing field, allowing all students to access high-quality test preparation.

Why All This Testing?

From a young age, American students encounter standardized testing on a regular basis. While secondary schools in many countries emphasize free-answer questions in exams, American children are trained to select the correct answer from four multiple-choice options. When applying to colleges, a high school student's standardized test scores can be a key metric in admissions decisions. This begs the question: why does American education place such a high value on standardized tests?

The answers lie in the structure of the American education system, which is built upon the principles of individual accountability and freedom of choice. As long as students receive a solid education, American schools and parents can choose how this goal is achieved. This autonomy in decision-making involves fifty states, thousands of school districts, and millions of parents. The result is a highly decentralized and variable educational landscape. Each state sets its minimum academic standards, school districts adopt unique curricula and requirements, and parents can choose from various schooling options, including homeschooling.

> The education system is highly decentralized

To obtain a high school diploma, American high school students do not have to pass centralized, final examinations like the A-Levels in Great Britain, the Baccalauréat in France, or the Abitur in Germany. Some students graduate by completing the minimum required classes and being present for four years, while others study at college-level standards. Yet, regardless of their approach, American students all graduate with a high school diploma. For example, in 2023, 56% of California high school graduates did not meet the A-G minimum requirements[21], meaning that one in two students could not even apply to a California public university. For these students, the only pathway for continuing their education is attending a community college with a potential transfer to a four-year institution later. This example illustrates that the high school diploma in itself is not a reliable measurement of academic aptitude or performance.

> The high school diploma has no central final exam

Standardized testing is a mechanism to bring transparency and comparability to a highly diverse education system that lacks a standard college readiness exam. Across the U.S., each state applies different curricula and graduation requirements, school districts face varying levels of funding and resources, and every high school educates all students, from those facing challenges to the most gifted ones. Some schools are rigorous in their assessments and grading, while others are more lenient or may allow grade inflation ('everyone gets an A'). Homeschooling adds even more variability as parents educate their children based on their individual standards and belief

> Standardized tests bring transparency into a highly diverse landscape

systems. This diversity makes it difficult to accurately assess whether a student's academic performance is as substantial as it might look on paper. Standardized testing provides a benchmark that allows for more accurate assessments.

Colleges use standardized tests to account for this educational variability; they establish a baseline. Test scores allow the admissions team to assess a student's academic performance in the context of the general applicant pool. Regardless of their schooling experience, all students sitting for the AP, SAT, and ACT exams take the same centralized tests, and their performance is comparable to their peers. Standardized testing allows colleges to gain objective insights into where an applicant's academic performance falls in the larger context. While they may not be perfect – as not all students have access to the same resources – standardized tests may be the most objective option to assess academic performance and potential.

> Standardized tests establish a baseline for all students

> The *No Child Left Behind Act* enforced standardized testing as a political measure

In addition to establishing a baseline, standardized testing has political roots. The *No Child Left Behind Act*, enacted in 2002 under President George W. Bush, represented a significant overhaul of federal educational policy. It aimed to give all American children a fair and equal opportunity for a high-quality education. The act was based on the belief that setting high standards and establishing measurable goals would improve individual outcomes. It mandated schools to meet specific educational benchmarks in reading, math, and science.

Standardized tests became a metric to assess a school's yearly progress, and schools that failed to meet their targets for consecutive years faced sanctions, including school closure. As a consequence, schools put increased emphasis on test preparation: under pressure to meet federal standards, schools often reallocated resources and instructional time to focus on test preparation, a practice known as 'teaching to the test.'

Critics argue that this led to a narrowing of the curriculum, with less time for subjects like science, social studies, and the arts. The act, however, did bring about some positive changes as it increased transparency in education by requiring schools to report detailed data on student performance and holding schools more accountable than in the past. In 2015, the NCLB Act was replaced by the *Every Student Succeeds Act*, which assigns more flexibility and funding while maintaining the focus on measuring student performance as a key metric.

Chapter 4 – The American College Landscape

Now that we have a better understanding of how American teenagers prepare for college, let us look closer at the U.S. college landscape. Most Americans use the terms college, school, and university interchangeably, and this handbook follows this common colloquial practice. However, technically, colleges and universities differ in their academic offerings, structure, and funding.

Types of Colleges

Research Universities

Research universities are large institutions focused on both teaching and research. They offer a broad range of undergraduate, graduate, and doctoral programs. One defining characteristic of universities is their strong emphasis on research and academic scholarship. Faculty members contribute to the advancement of knowledge through research in addition to their teaching responsibilities. Professors and graduate students are actively engaged in research projects, and even undergraduate students may have opportunities to participate.

-Teaching
-Research
-Graduate programs

Universities typically have extensive facilities and well-established partnerships with industries and government agencies.

Many universities have tens of thousands of students enrolled. In 2023, over 77,000 students were enrolled at Texas A&M[22], the largest university campus in the United States. Often, universities break down their institution into smaller 'schools' or 'colleges' to give their large student body a more personal experience. These divisions operate within the university's framework and focus on a specific field, such as the sciences, law, or business, or aim to provide a particular campus experience, like the international house.

> Universities are organized in divisions called schools or colleges (e.g. College of Engineering)

Another way to cultivate a more intimate academic environment is through honors colleges or programs that offer an enriched educational experience for high-achieving students. These programs are characterized by a commitment to academic rigor, small class sizes, and a focus on intellectual curiosity. Some experts compare honors programs with a private school environment within a public institution. The honors curriculum usually fosters interdisciplinary exploration, and honors students may enjoy exclusive privileges, such as priority course registration, direct access to research projects, or dedicated seminars not available to the general student population. Upon admission, select students may be invited to apply to the university's honors program.

> Honors colleges offer small class sizes and other perks

Colleges

In their original definition, colleges are smaller institutions with fewer students than universities focused on undergraduate programs. While some colleges may offer limited graduate programs, their primary mission is to provide a well-rounded undergraduate experience. Colleges usually have smaller class sizes than research universities, allowing them to provide a more intimate learning environment that

> Colleges focus on undergraduate programs

encourages lively class discussions, personalized attention, and a sense of community. Faculty members may have fewer research responsibilities than university professors. Some colleges refer to themselves as 'college' but function more like a university, offering various programs and intensively engaging in research activities.

As a special variation, liberal arts colleges take a broader approach to education, emphasizing critical thinking, communication, and problem-solving skills. While they traditionally focused on the humanities, many liberal arts colleges have expanded their programs to include STEM degrees. Students typically take various arts, humanity, language, and sciences classes, allowing them to explore many different fields before deciding on a major. At liberal arts colleges, 50% to 75% of classes may be outside of a student's declared major.

> Liberal arts colleges focus on the humanities and academic exploration

Some students decide to begin their college experience at local community or junior colleges, which offer two-year programs leading to associate degrees or professional certificates. Community colleges provide affordable education to many students, including those seeking career-oriented programs or planning to transfer to a four-year institution later. Instead of a complex admissions process, community colleges usually admit all students with a high school diploma. While some students explore vocational or technical programs, others aim to knock out their general education and lower-division requirements before transferring to a more expensive 4-year college.

By taking introductory courses at a cheaper institution, students can significantly reduce the overall cost of their bachelor's degree. In addition, many community colleges have transfer agreements with four-year institutions. For instance, every year, about 80,000 students obtain their associate degree at a California community college, allowing them to transfer seamlessly to a UC or CSU[23].

The American College System

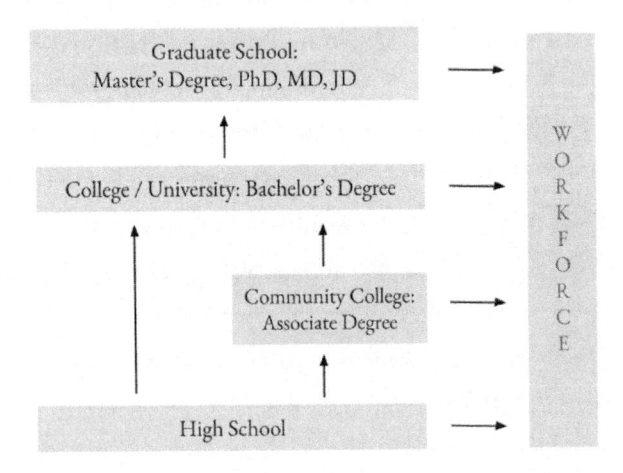

```
                Graduate School:              →
          Master's Degree, PhD, MD, JD
                       ↑                          W
                                                  O
                                                  R
       College / University: Bachelor's Degree →  K
                                                  F
              ↑            ↑                      O
                                                  R
                     Community College:        →  C
                     Associate Degree             E
                           ↑
                      High School              →
```

Public versus Private Institutions

How an institution finances its operations is a crucial factor that influences various aspects of its functioning, including tuition rates, institutional priorities, and educational programs offered. This is particularly evident in the contrasting financial models employed by public and private colleges. Public universities receive a substantial portion of their funding from taxpayers and government sources, which significantly reduces their operational expenses. This financial support from public sources enables public universities to offer lower tuition rates than private ones. However, public universities typically differentiate their tuition rates based on residency status. Since in-state students contribute to public education through tax payments, they benefit from substantially lower tuition fees than out-of-state and international students. Some colleges impose additional surcharges ranging from a few hundred to thousands of dollars for international students to cover incremental services.

> Public institutions are funded by taxes and tuition

Unlike public universities, private colleges rely on tuition fees, endowments, and private donations as their primary sources of funding. With limited or no direct government subsidies, private institutions typically charge higher tuition rates across the board, regardless of a student's residency status. Research universities may secure additional funding through research grants, often provided by federal agencies, private foundations, or industry partners. These grants support research projects and contribute to the

> Private colleges are funded by tuition and endowments

institution's overall budget. While most colleges receive philanthropic contributions, private institutions often have substantial endowments through their alumni network and various foundations. For example, the size of Harvard's endowment was $50.7 billion[24] in 2023 – as large as the gross domestic product of a small country!

Residential versus Commuter Schools

Campus life is another crucial aspect of higher education that can influence a student's social, personal, and academic growth. Different types of institutions offer varied campus experiences. Most 4-year colleges provide a traditional residential college experience with on-campus dormitories, dining facilities, various clubs, athletic amenities, and a vibrant campus life. American college campuses often resemble self-contained towns, complete with their own infrastructure.

> Residential, commuter, and online colleges provide unique campus experiences

Some colleges are infamous for their social life, while others offer a more balanced approach. For many students, the on-campus college experience is a bridge into adulthood, a place where they can spread their wings and become independent and responsible adults.

Yet this traditional model does not fit everyone, and many students choose a different college experience that aligns better with their needs. Some students attend a nearby commuter school for personal or cost reasons. Smaller state schools and community colleges often cater to students living off-campus and commuting to attend classes. While this model saves the costs for room and board, it can limit socializing

Chapter 4— The American College Landscape

opportunities. With the rise of online education, some institutions have specialized in offering degree programs entirely online or in a hybrid model that combines online with on-campus classes. These colleges provide flexibility for non-traditional students, allowing them to balance education with work or other commitments.

For-Profit Schools

While most American colleges are non-profit organizations, over 250 for-profit institutions grant four-year degrees[25]. Non-profit institutions reinvest any potential financial gains in their educational programs. For-profit schools, however, are businesses that distribute their profits among their investors instead of reinvesting in education. They often have higher acceptance rates and may charge less than private non-profit colleges, but typically are more expensive than public institutions. The main drawbacks of for-profit schools are their low graduation rates and potential accreditation issues.

For-profit colleges may face accreditation issues

The Ivy League

When talking about American college education, most people immediately think of Harvard and Yale, both renowned for their academic excellence and prestigious reputation. Exploring the American college landscape inevitably involves mentioning the Ivy League, a group of colleges that some consider a class in itself. The Ivies consistently rank among the most prestigious institutions in the world and carry a reputation for producing global leaders across various fields.

Harvard University, established in 1636, holds the title of the oldest Ivy, with the other members founded in the 18th and 19th centuries. While today, we think of the Ivies as a beacon of academic excellence and prestige, they started as an athletic league. Harvard and Yale engaged in their first collegiate rowing race in 1852, sparking interest in competitive sports among other colleges and leading to the Intercollegiate Rowing Association. The term 'Ivy League' was coined in the 1930s when the athletic conference formalized its structure and included other sports.

> The Ivies are known for their prestige and highly selective admissions process

Today, the Ivy League is synonymous with academic excellence, boasting renowned faculty, rigorous programs, and a commitment to research. At the same time, these colleges are known for their hefty price tag and low acceptance rates. The Ivies consistently lead the national and global university rankings. Their prestige extends beyond academia, potentially influencing career trajectories through their extensive network of influential alumni. For most high school students, the Ivies are known for their highly selective admissions process. Their single-digit acceptance rates reinforce our perception of their elite status.

> **The Ivy League:**
> Brown, Columbia, Cornell, Dartmouth, Harvard, U. of Pennsylvania, Princeton, and Yale

Chapter 4— The American College Landscape

In the past 20 years, Harvard's acceptance rate has dropped from 9.8% in 2002[26] to 3.5% in 2023[27]. While they received just over 19,000 applications in 2002, this number exploded to over 56,000 applicants in 2023, with only 1,966 students admitted[28] (15% of those were international students). As the number of slots for Harvard's first-year class did not change, the explosion in applications drove down their acceptance rate.

The math is easy: increase the number of applying students while keeping the number of available slots constant, and you end up with a lower acceptance rate. As long as the Ivies receive more and more applications every year, their selectivity, measured in a low acceptance rate, increases. This phenomenon is not unique to the Ivies but is also noticeable in other highly selective colleges with admit rates under 20%, such as Stanford University or MIT. This begs the question of what fuels this trend of increasing applications, and what it means for college admissions.

> Acceptance rates at the Ivies dropped to single digits

Driving Selectivity through an Influx of Applications

In recent years, the number of applications received by colleges, particularly highly selective ones, has skyrocketed. Several factors catapulted the number of applications to new levels, including marketing campaigns, the digitalization of the application process, and the implementation of test-optional policies.

In the past 20 years, colleges have ramped up their marketing efforts, reaching out directly to prospective students. Once a student takes the

PSAT, SAT, or AP exam, their contact information becomes a valuable commodity. By purchasing their addresses and demographics for just $0.45 per name[29], colleges can reach out directly to prospective applicants. They inundate students with emails and fancy marketing brochures, advertising their academic programs and inviting them to apply. A larger applicant pool allows colleges to lower their acceptance rates, which is the standard metric for prestige. Often, selective colleges encourage applications from candidates who may not have a competitive profile for admissions, a practice known as 'recruit to deny.'

Direct marketing campaigns proved to be an effective way to entice flattered teenagers to apply to colleges that are unlikely to admit them. The increasingly competitive admissions process also fueled a sense of urgency among students, prompting them to apply to more colleges than previous generations. This phenomenon has led to the standard recommendation for students to apply to at least twelve colleges. The Ivies and other top colleges have taken this marketing tactic a step further by adopting a global marketing approach. Through targeted campaigns, they seek to expand their applicant pool beyond the United States, tapping into the growing number of talented students from around the world.

> Direct marketing increases the number of applications

The surge in college applications would not have been possible without the digital version of the Common App. In the traditional method, students had to manually fill out separate paper applications for each college and

> The digital version of the Common App facilitated an increase in applications

physically mail them. When the Common App became fully digital in 2007, it revolutionized college applications for both applicants and admissions offices. The streamlined digital process allows students to apply to multiple colleges with just a few clicks, significantly increasing the number of colleges they can apply to.

More recently, the pandemic has propelled application numbers to new heights. In response to the challenges posed by the pandemic, during which many students could not take standardized tests, most colleges adopted test-optional admissions policies. Under these policies, applicants were no longer required to submit standardized test scores, such as the SAT or ACT, as part of their application. While the switch to test-optional policies was intended to provide flexibility and alleviate stress for applicants, it led to an unintended consequence: a significant increase in the number of applications. Without the perceived barrier of achieving a minimum score on their standardized tests, more students felt encouraged to apply, contributing to the surge in applications.

> Test-optional policies fueled an explosion in applications

This phenomenon was particularly pronounced at highly selective colleges. Many students reasoned that since Harvard or Yale was sending them a brochure encouraging them to apply without the need to include test scores, they might as well submit an application. Yet, when more applicants apply for the same number of available spots, a college's acceptance rate decreases and their selectivity increases. Not surprisingly, many colleges saw a sharp decline in their admission rates after introducing test-optional policies, fueled by the increase in applications. In 2007, applicants to UC Berkeley had a 23.3% chance of admission, but by 2023, this rate had halved to 11.7%[30]. For the most selective colleges, acceptance rates plummeted even more. By 2023, Harvard's rate had dropped to 3.4%, a third of its 2007 rate of 9.8%[31].

Are Ivy League Colleges Worthwhile?

Our society places a high value on prestige, and Ivy League colleges underline their prestigious status with single-digit admission rates. Attending an Ivy can be life-changing, an argument often made by alumni, but it may not be a good fit for everyone. While the Ivies League offers a wealth of academic resources and access to a powerful alumni network, other factors such as fit, personal priorities, and potential return on investment must also be considered.

> Ivies offer prestige and networking but come with high costs and intense competition

A college's reputation can be important in specific fields, such as investment banking, consulting, law, and academia. However, for most professions, graduating from a prestigious brand-name college is not a make-or-break factor. The question of whether they are truly worthwhile depends on one's unique goals and circumstances. There is no standard answer, but here are some thoughts to consider.

> Cost of attending an Ivy can be over $80,000 per year

An important aspect is the potential return on investment, which is determined by the cost of attendance and potential earnings after graduation. Attending an Ivy League often exceeds $80,000 annually, and despite generous financial aid programs, high cost of

Chapter 4— The American College Landscape

attendance remains a barrier for many applicants. Particularly, middle-class families who do not qualify for need-based aid may find themselves unable to afford full-price tuition. In 2022, alumni from MIT and Harvey-Mudd College, both not members of the Ivy League, had the highest starting and mid-career earnings, with Princeton ranking in third place[32]. Given their high tuition rates, the return on investment for Ivies may be lower than for more affordable public universities. While most of us would not buy a house or a car without a detailed, rational cost analysis, we may not apply the same level of scrutiny in college applications. Many families consider expensive college options without verifying their potential for future payoff.

Furthermore, American society attaches a high emotional value to the Ivies and other brand-name colleges. We equate a college with higher selectivity with higher value and, by extension, our own self-worth. Prestigious colleges are nicknamed 'sweater schools,' as students and their families proudly wear shirts displaying the college name. Ivy League colleges are often idealized as a symbol of the American Dream. In a society based on merit, everyone has the same opportunities, and it is up to the individual to be the agent of their good fortune.

This narrative, however, is challenged by the prevalence of legacy admissions, where applicants with family members who attended the same college often receive preferential treatment. A recent study by a Harvard research group found that children of alumni have a 37% chance of admission to their parents' alma mater, compared to only 9.5% for non-legacy applicants with a similar academic profile[33]. In addition, institutional priorities and the

> Admissions to the Ivy League may not be based on merit alone

desire to maintain a particular academic and social balance in their student body can influence admissions decisions, further evidence that admissions may not be based on merit alone.

In their pursuit of attending a highly prestigious college, some students apply exclusively to Ivy League and other competitive institutions. However, this approach carries a significant risk due to the extremely limited number of available spots. With acceptance rates below 20%, these so-called 'Ivy plus schools' are effectively reach schools for all applicants, regardless of their academic qualifications. As a result, even stellar students who apply exclusively to ultra-competitive colleges may find themselves without any admission offer, forcing them to explore alternative paths. To mitigate this risk, students should create a balanced college list that includes colleges with higher admission rates.

> Colleges with admit rates below 20% are reach schools for all applicants

There is no universal answer to whether the Ivie League colleges are worthwhile, and each student needs to consider their own priorities and circumstances when finding their answer. While the Ivies provide stellar academics and opportunities, they certainly do not own this privilege. Students can get an excellent education at most, if not all, American colleges. At the end of the day, your college experience is determined by how much you make out of it, not by the college name.

> College is what you make of it

Chapter 4— The American College Landscape

U.S. College Rankings

The U.S. News & World Report published the first-ever ranking of American colleges in 1993. In the 1990s, peer interviews with university presidents or deans decided where a school ended up on the list, but over time, the report included more quantifiable criteria. Today, this annual report is considered the gold standard for assessing higher education and emphasizes student outcomes and institutional effectiveness.

-Acceptance rates
-GPA & test scores
-Retention rate
-Graduation rate
-Social mobility
-Diversity
-Student debt
-Peer review

Student success, like enrollment, retention, graduation, and manageable debt, account for half of the report's ranking criteria[34]. One of the newest variables measured is 'social mobility,' which considers the graduation rates of low-income students or those who are the first in their families to attend a 4-year college. The goal is to evaluate the institution's effectiveness in providing educational opportunities for students from diverse economic and social backgrounds. Faculty resources, including salaries, student-faculty ratio, full-time faculty, and financial resources, are additional ranking criteria, as well as standardized test scores of incoming students.

Despite efforts to base college rankings on measurable data, subjective peer assessments still weigh with 20% in today's formula. The report asks university presidents, deans, or other faculty members to assess their fellow institutions. While interviews offer an insider perspective, peer assessment is highly subjective and not based on quantifiable data.

Recognizing the significance of these rankings, colleges adjust their institutional priorities to correspond with the ranking criteria used to evaluate them. The factors that drive a college's ranking directly shape the admissions process. For example, as current rankings increasingly emphasize student diversity, colleges have responded by admitting more students from diverse backgrounds. The criteria used for the college rankings directly shape the demographic makeup of a college's student body. Like in business, you get what you measure.

While it is obvious why colleges aim to perform well in rankings, why do we, prospective students, families, and society, attribute so much value to a list of top 100 universities? In the complex world of American colleges, rankings appeal to us as they establish a social order and seem to answer the question of quality. The list of top 100 colleges provides an easy answer to a complex problem. However, oversimplified answers do not tell the whole story and may not be the best guide for one's personal goals. There are 4,000 degree-granting institutions[35] in the United States, yet many applicants apply to only the same brand names.

> Rankings influence a college's prestige, their priorities, and application numbers

Dissecting the landscape of thousands of institutions to find those that fit us best seems like a Sisyphean task, so we welcome the rankings as a quick shortcut. By doing so, we may set ourselves up for failure due to the high selectivity of these colleges or by neglecting our individual fit. Less-known colleges may not make it on the ranking but can offer a better fit for our specific needs. Therefore, keeping an open mind when crafting one's college list is essential.

Chapter 4— The American College Landscape

U.S. Degrees

Undergraduate Degrees

American college degrees range from associate to doctoral degrees, each representing distinct levels of academic achievement and expertise. Associate's degrees are two-year programs at community colleges that provide a practical and cost-effective way to begin college or gain useful skills for immediate entry into the workforce. Degrees like the Associate of Arts and Associate of Science lay a general education foundation with introductory coursework in a specific field.

AA and AS are 2-year degrees

Bachelor's degrees, such as the Bachelor of Arts (BA), Bachelor of Science (BS), and Bachelor of Fine Arts (BFA) are undergraduate degrees awarded by four-year colleges. The BA typically emphasizes a broader liberal arts education across humanities and social sciences, while the BS focuses on scientific or technical fields. Students fulfill general education requirements, major coursework, and electives to earn a well-rounded undergraduate education and a predetermined number of credits in their major.

BA, BS, and BFA are 4-year programs

As the primary field of study, the major shapes a student's core curriculum. Students declare a major when applying to college or during their first or second year. Many institutions permit students to

Major = primary field of study

switch majors during the first two years, and liberal arts programs encourage exploring various subjects before committing to a major after the second year.

Most programs offer multiple options to customize one's major through electives, minors, concentrations, and double majoring in a second area. This flexibility enables students to explore additional interests, develop a broader skill set, or specialize further within their major field. A minor provides an optional secondary specialization requiring fewer courses than a major. Students can diversify their profile by adding a minor, appealing to a broader range of employers or graduate programs. The adaptability of American degrees allows students to tailor their education to their interests and career goals.

> Minor = optional secondary field of study

Graduate Programs

After completing their undergraduate studies, many students pursue an advanced degree, allowing them to specialize in their chosen field. Graduate programs lead to a master's or doctoral degree and provide in-depth knowledge and preparation for advanced career roles, academia, or research. The Master of Arts (MA) and the Master of Science (MS) range from one to three years of study, and students undertake advanced coursework, conduct research, and often complete a thesis or pass a comprehensive exam.

> Master's: MA, MS
> Doctoral degrees: PhD, MD, JD, Ed. D

Chapter 4— The American College Landscape

Doctoral degrees, such as Doctor of Philosophy (PhD), Medical Doctor (MD), Doctorate in Education (Ed. D), and Juris Doctor (JD) represent the highest level of academic achievement. They typically include three or more years of coursework, comprehensive exams, and completing an original research project, the doctoral dissertation.

Applicants must have a bachelor's degree or equivalent from an accredited institution to apply for graduate school, and some programs may specify a degree in a specific field or coursework prerequisites. While some are test-optional, many graduate programs require test scores from the graduate record examination[36]. The GRE is a standardized test that measures verbal reasoning, quantitative reasoning, and analytical writing skills. Students can take it at one of the 1,000 test centers worldwide or online at home.

> Grad school application: bachelor's, GPA, GRE/LSAT/ MCAT scores, statement of purpose

Applicants must also provide two to three letters of recommendation, ideally from faculty or professionals familiar with their academic performance and potential for graduate study. They must also submit a 'statement of purpose,' an essay outlining their academic interests, professional goals, and reasons for pursuing a graduate degree in their chosen field. Official transcripts from all undergraduate and postgraduate institutions attended must also be submitted in the application. International students whose first language is not English may need to submit TOEFL or IELTS scores to demonstrate their English proficiency.

Specifics of Medical and Law Schools

Let us begin with a word of caution for medicine and law. Both fields must follow distinct licensing processes, which can be challenging to transfer to other countries later. U.S. physicians must be licensed in the state where they intend to practice and pass the United States Medical Licensing Examination.

> U.S. medical and law degrees may not transfer to other countries

However, the transferability of this exam to other countries varies. In addition to potential licensing issues, very few slots are available at medical schools for international students. Along the same lines, international students considering law school must assess potential licensing issues. State-specific requirements govern legal practice in the United States, and lawyers must be admitted to the Bar Association of each state where they wish to practice. The Bar exams are specific to the U.S. legal system and might not apply to other countries. Assuming that international students have thoroughly assessed these licensing issues, let us examine the specifics of medical and law schools in the States.

Medical School

Medical school is a specialized path for aspiring physicians and involves several key stages. Students must complete specific prerequisite courses during their undergraduate education before applying to medical school. While no specific major requirement exists, aspiring medical students often pursue

> A bachelor's degree, excellent grades & MCAT scores

undergraduate degrees in biology, chemistry, or specific pre-med programs. In addition to obtaining an undergraduate degree, students must take the Medical College Admission Test[37], a standardized exam that assesses knowledge of natural, behavioral, and social science concepts. The MCAT score and academic performance are crucial components of the application to medical school.

Once accepted, med school typically lasts four years and is divided into two phases: pre-clinical and clinical. Pre-clinical years focus on classroom-based learning and cover fundamental medical sciences. The clinical years involve hands-on training in hospitals and clinics, providing practical experience in patient care. After graduating from medical school, individuals enter residency to gain practical experience in a specific medical field. Residency programs can last three to seven years, depending on the specialty. Board certification exams follow the completion of residency in the chosen specialty. Physicians must obtain a medical license in the state where they plan to practice and must pass the USMLE, which assesses their ability to apply general medical knowledge. Some doctors pursue further specialization through fellowships, expanding their expertise in specific areas of medicine.

> Med school spans 4 years, followed by residency (3-7 years) and USMLE board licensing

Law School

Law school is the path for individuals aiming to become legal professionals, including lawyers, judges, and attorneys. Like medical school, attending law school involves several steps. First, applicants complete a bachelor's degree in any field, with political science, history, or business being popular pre-law majors. However, some law schools have specific prerequisite courses that applicants must take during their undergraduate program. The Law School Admission Test[38] is a standardized test that assesses reading and verbal reasoning skills. Until now, the LSAT held the monopoly to apply to law school. However, the American Bar Association recently approved the GRE as an alternative to the LSAT for applications starting in 2025[39].

Law school spans three years, during which students study fundamental legal principles and gain practical skills. The first year typically covers foundational courses, while the second and third years allow for specialization through elective courses. Upon completion of law school, students are awarded a Juris Doctor degree. To practice law, graduates must pass the Bar Examination, which tests state-specific and general legal principles. Afterwards, they may pursue careers in various legal specialties or work in law firms, government agencies, or corporations.

> Law school spans 3 years, followed by the Bar Exam

Chapter 5 – California's Three-Tier Model

Who does not dream of year-round sunshine and surfing the Pacific waves during their college years? California is not only the state with the largest population but also ranks high on the college lists of many out-of-state and international students. The State of California offers multiple pathways through its three-tier model, demonstrating its commitment to accessible and affordable education. While the University of California Berkeley is a well-known institution worldwide, California's public education system offers many more options, including community colleges, the California State University, and the University of California.

California Community Colleges

The 116 community colleges[40] are the base of California's higher education system. These colleges offer two-year associate degree programs and various transfer opportunities to four-year institutions. In 2022, about 1.8 million students studied at a community college; 59% pursued a two- or four-year degree, and 62% were part-time students[41]. As community

> 1.8 million students attend one of the 116 community colleges in California

colleges do not offer on-campus housing, they are the prototype of a commuter college, with students living either with their families or in off-campus arrangements. What community colleges may lack in vibrant campus life, they make up for in accessibility and affordability, allowing people from all walks of life to attend. Many community colleges offer in-person, online, and hybrid classes, giving students great flexibility.

Community colleges offer numerous advantages. Since they are open to all high school graduates, they offer a pathway to a four-year institution for students who might otherwise not have this opportunity. Up to 80,000 community college students transfer to a CSU or UC every year – this is a well-established path.

Affordable and flexible pathway to 4-year universities

Another benefit of community colleges is their affordability. For California residents, community colleges offer reduced tuition through the *California College Promise Program*, and some colleges even waive tuition altogether for first-time local college students. Some cost benefits also apply to out-of-state and international students. For example, tuition at Foothill College[1], California's top-ranked community college[42], is about $16,000 for international students[43]. Non-resident annual tuition at CalPoly in San Luis Obispo costs about $23,700[44], while the University of California charges about $53,500[45] tuition per year.

---

[1] Annual tuition estimates are based on three quarters with 16 credits each, including fees and student health insurance. Excludes room & board and personal expenses.

Chapter 5— California's Three-Tier Model

The 2+2 program offers students an affordable pathway to obtain a bachelor's degree from a California State University or University of California campus. Students begin by attending a community college for the first two years, benefiting from lower tuition rates. During this time, they complete most general education requirements and some lower-division major courses, earning them an associate's degree for transfer. Then, they transfer to a CSU or UC to finish the remaining two years of coursework. Since pre-approved classes cover the same content as lower-division courses at a CSU or UC, students transfer right into their third year with equivalent knowledge as those who started there. As long as all requirements are met, such as maintaining a minimum GPA, students can transfer up to 90 credits. In addition, the *Transfer Admission Guarantee*[46] assures admission to a specific participating UC campus for qualified students. Upon graduation, transfer students receive their degrees from the CSU or UC, just like those who attended for all four years.

Despite the many benefits of community colleges, a word of caution is warranted. When planning to transfer to a private college or an institution outside of California, students must thoroughly research the transfer policies of the target college to ensure all completed courses will be accepted. Some colleges, particularly private ones, may not accept all classes taken at a community college, especially if the community college is on the quarter system but the target institution uses academic semesters.

> Verify which credits can be transferred to private and out-of-state colleges

Keep also in mind that community colleges have limited research opportunities, which present both advantages and disadvantages. On the positive side, all classes are taught by professors rather than graduate students or teaching assistants since community colleges do not engage in extensive research activities. Many professors choose to work at a community college due to their passion for teaching and direct interaction with students. However, the drawback of this teaching-focused environment is the lack of research programs typically found at four-year institutions, making it more difficult to gain research experience at a community college.

The California State University

The California State University is the nation's largest four-year public university system, comprised of 23 campuses and enrolling about 460,000 students[47]. Positioned as the mid-tier option within California's public higher education system, the 23 CSU campuses offer many undergraduate and graduate programs across liberal arts, sciences, engineering, education, business, and other disciplines.

> 460,000 students at 23 campuses

> CSUs are known for their hands-on learning

The CSUs are renowned for emphasizing practical, hands-on learning that prepares students for their future careers. Through internships, cooperative education programs, and service-learning projects, students can apply classroom concepts to real-world scenarios, gaining practical skills and work experience in collaboration

Chapter 5— California's Three-Tier Model

with industry partners. Among the 23 campuses, several are recognized as flagship institutions for specific programs. San Diego State University, San Jose State University, and Cal Poly San Luis Obispo are particularly known for their strong Engineering and Computer Science programs.

The California State University

- Humboldt
- Chico
- Sonoma
- Sacramento
- Maritime
- San Francisco
- East Bay
- San Jose
- Stanislaus
- Fresno
- Monterey Bay
- Bakersfield
- San Luis Obispo
- Northridge
- Channel Islands
- San Bernardino
- Los Angeles
- Pomona
- Dominguez Hills
- Fullerton
- Long Beach
- San Diego
- San Marcos

Admissions Requirements

To be eligible to apply to a CSU[48], high school students must complete a minimum of 15 units of specified 'A-G' courses. These include history/social science, English, math, laboratory science, foreign language, visual and performing arts, and an additional college preparatory elective. The CSUs award extra points for approved honors,

IB, and AP courses taken in the last three years of high school, with a maximum of eight semesters considered. Extra points are based on the grades earned in these advanced courses when recalculating the overall GPA. California residents need a minimum GPA of 2.50 for admission, while non-residents require a GPA of at least 3.00. Applicants living in the same county as the target CSU campus receive an additional bump of 0.25 points in their recalculated GPA.

For impacted majors and campuses[49], supplemental factors like the GPA in math and sciences, the number of math and English courses taken beyond the minimum, extracurriculars, leadership involvement, or household income may be reviewed alongside the A-G GPA. International applicants must demonstrate English proficiency by providing TOEFL scores of at least 500 (paper-based) or 61 (internet-based)[50]. Some CSUs may require higher scores or accept the IELTS test – always check the requirements for your target campus.

> Admission is based on GPA, activities, and demographics

The California State University has adopted a test-blind admissions policy, which means that they do not consider SAT or ACT scores during the application process. However, these scores can be used for course placement after acceptance. The CSU application is unique in that it does not require essays or letters of recommendations and only considers demographics, academics, and the activity list for admissions.

> The CSUs are test-blind and require no essays or letters of recommendation

Chapter 5— California's Three-Tier Model

As a tax-funded public university, the California State University prioritizes California residents over out-of-state and international applicants. If a transfer applicant from a California community college is denied from their preferred campus, they may be redirected to an alternative CSU[51]. For more details about the CSU application, refer to their online application guide[52].

The University of California

The University of California is the top tier of California's higher education system. UC campuses are renowned for their academic excellence and research, offering 850 undergraduate, graduate, and professional degree programs in various disciplines. The UC system boasts an impressive track record with 70 Nobel Prize winners, over 13,300 patents, and 1,500 startup businesses launched using UC intellectual property[53].

290,000 students

70 Nobel Prize winners

The University of California has ten campuses with unique offerings and vibes. UC Santa Barbara and UC San Diego are right next to the Pacific shoreline, UC Santa Cruz is nestled in a redwood forest overlooking the ocean, and UC Berkeley and UC San Francisco are urban campuses. While most campuses house both undergraduate and graduate students, offers the campus in San Francisco only graduate programs. The UC system is home to approximately 230,000

9 UCs for graduate and undergraduate studies

UCSF: graduate programs

undergraduate and 63,000 graduate students. Most campuses educate over 20,000 students, with UCLA, UCB, and UCSD each having over 40,000 enrolled students. UC Merced is the newest campus, which opened in 2005.

The University of California

- UC Davis
- UC Berkeley
- UC San Francisco
- UC Santa Cruz
- UC Merced
- UC Santa Barbara
- UC Los Angeles
- UC Riverside
- UC Irvine
- UC San Diego

UC Berkeley is renowned for its rigorous academics and consistently ranks among the top public universities in the world. UCLA emphasizes research but adds a strong focus on the performing arts and film, thanks to its proximity to Hollywood. UC San Diego excels in STEM fields, while UC Davis is renowned for its agricultural sciences and veterinary medicine. All nine undergraduate campuses are ranked in the top 100 national[54] and public colleges[55], with UC Berkeley and UCLA tied for

Chapter 5— California's Three-Tier Model

the number one spot as the highest-ranked public universities in the United States.

	National College Ranking	Public College Ranking
UC Berkeley	# 15	# 1
UCLA	# 15	# 1
UC Davis	# 28	# 6
UC San Diego	# 28	# 6
UC Irvine	# 33	# 10
UC Santa Barbara	# 35	# 12
UC Merced	# 60	# 28
UC Riverside	# 76	# 36
UC Santa Cruz	#82	# 40

Source: U.S. News College Rankings 2024

A-G Admissions Requirements

Like the CSU, the UC system utilizes the A-G requirements[56] to ensure incoming students are well prepared for university-level work. The A-G designation refers to seven core academic areas students must complete in high school. The UC recalculates a student's GPA based solely on their A-G courses taken during grades ten and eleven. To be eligible for admission, California applicants must have a minimum recalculated GPA of 3.0, while out-of-state and international students need at least a recalculated GPA of 3.4.

Admissions to the University of California is highly competitive, with over 250,000 applications in 2024[57]. Students are strongly advised to strive for the highest possible GPA during grades ten and eleven. Applicants must complete at least eleven of the fifteen required courses before their senior year; only up to four courses may be taken in grade twelve. The UC website provides an online tool listing all approved A-G courses for California high schools[58].

Minimum A-G course requirements:

- 2 years of history or social science
- 4 years of English
- 3 years of math, including algebra 1, geometry, and algebra 2
- 2 years of laboratory science (biology, chemistry, or physics)
- 2 years of the same foreign language
- 1 year in visual and performing arts
- 1 year of elective coursework

Recalculating the High School GPA

Most colleges recalculate an applicant's GPA using their own specific formula. This process helps to standardize GPAs across different high schools and grading scales, allowing for consistent comparison of academic records. Some colleges remove weighted grades, while others convert submitted GPAs to their own scale. Admissions offices may include only core academic courses in the recalculation or factor in electives and

> The UCs only consider the A-G grades from 10th and 11th grade

Chapter 5— California's Three-Tier Model

non-academic subjects as well. GPA trends over time are also often assessed (hint: they want to see an upward trajectory).

The University of California system is very transparent about its formula for recalculating GPAs. They only factor in the grades of approved A-G courses during sophomore and junior years, making strong academic performance in these two years absolutely critical.

Step-by-step instructions to derive the recalculated UC GPA:

Step 1: Convert the letter grades in all A-G courses completed in 10th and 11th grade. A=4 points, B=3 points, C=2 points, D=1 point. Pluses and minuses are not considered. Subjects outside the A-G requirements are also not considered.

Step 2: Add an extra point for each semester of a UC honors-level course, with a maximum of 8 semester points between 10th and 11th grades; a maximum of 4 semesters can be from 10th grade. For California residents, honors courses include AP, IB Higher Level, designated IB Standard Level, UC-transferable college courses, and UC-certified honors courses[59]. Non-resident applicants receive the extra point only for AP or IB courses with a letter grade of A, B, or C.

Step 3: Add all the points to find your total grade points.

Step 4: Divide your total grade points by the number of letter grades earned in A-G courses taken in 10th and 11th grade. This calculation yields your UC-specific GPA (for example, 3.57). Do not round up or down.

The University of California caps the number of advanced classes that count toward the recalculated GPA formula at eight semester-long courses. This effectively means that only up to four year-long AP courses can boost the recalculated GPA. The capped formula determines whether an applicant is eligible to apply to a UC campus. However, to be competitive in the evaluation process, the UC admissions website strongly advises students to exceed the minimum requirements 'by large margins,'[60] especially when applying to the more competitive campuses. During the evaluation process, admissions officers may use the student's recalculated GPA as well as self-reported courses and grades based on the transcript. By comparing UC campus-specific admission statistics[61], which include the GPAs of previously admitted students, you can gauge how competitive your profile is.

The University of California also allows students to satisfy specific A-G subject requirements by achieving minimum scores on standardized tests[62]. Scoring well on APs, ACT, or other approved assessments can validate a student's competencies and fulfill A-G requirements when high school course options are limited. For example, scoring three or higher on an AP Calculus exam can satisfy two years of the mathematics requirement (excluding geometry), and an ACT English score of 24 fulfills three years of the English A-G requirement. Scoring at least 30 on the ACT English section or three or higher on an AP English Language/Literature exam fully satisfies the four-year A-G requirement for English.

> Minimum test scores can satisfy A-G requirements

Chapter 5— California's Three-Tier Model

International Requirements

Applicants who are not U.S. citizens or permanent residents and those with a non-immigrant visa are considered international students. The UC has modified its admissions criteria[63] for these students, including adapted A-G course requirements, country-specific provisions, and requesting proof of English language proficiency.

> International students = applicants who are not U.S. citizens or permanent residents

For students graduating from a non-U.S. high school after 13 years, coursework from that additional year should be entered under 12th grade, working backward through 11th and 10th grade levels.

> Some countries have specific admissions criteria

The University of California system has specific admissions criteria for applicants from Canada, China, Hong Kong, India, Indonesia, Korea, Malaysia, New Zealand, Pakistan, Saudi Arabia, and Singapore. Students enrolled in secondary schools following the British system and those attending an international or IB school abroad also have specific requirements. The UC website provides the most up-to-date requirements for all international applicants[64].

For all other applicants, the following table provides an overview of the A-G admissions requirements for American. and international students.

MISSION: ACCEPTED!

A-G Admission requirements: U.S. versus (most) international students[65]

		U. S. Students[66]	International Students[67]
Minimum GPA		3.0	3.4
A	History / Social Science	2 years of history or social science, including one year of world history and one year of US history or 1/2 year of US history and 1/2 year of civics or government	2 years of history of the home country
B	English	4 years of English composition and literature coursework	4 years of composition and literature in the language in which you are instructed
C	Math	3 years of college preparatory math, including algebra 1, geometry, and algebra 2	3 years of math, including elementary and advanced algebra and 2- and 3-dimensional geometry
D	Laboratory Science	2 years of lab science in at least two: biology, chemistry, and physics	2 years of science in two of these three subjects: biology, chemistry, or physics
E	Foreign language	2 years in the same language other than English	2 years of a second language
F	Arts	1 year in art, dance, drama/theater, or music	1 year of arts
G	Electives	1 additional year of 'A-F' subject area, computer science, advanced math, or AP courses	1 additional year-long course from any subject area above

English Proficiency

If international students attend a high school where the language of instruction is not English, they must provide evidence of their language proficiency– after all, students must be able to do their academic coursework in English! The UC generally accepts the following test scores to demonstrate this proficiency, but some campuses may require higher scores or an interview to confirm proficiency. Always verify the minimum language requirements for each campus before applying.

Minimum test scores demonstrating English proficiency:

Test	Minimum Score
ACT English Language Art	24+
SAT Writing and Language	31+
AP English Language/Composition or AP English Literature/Composition	3, 4, or 5
IB English Standard-Level examination	6 or 7
IB English Higher-Level examination	5, 6, or 7
IELTS	6.5+
TOEFL internet, iBT Home Edition, or iBT Paper Edition only	80+
Duolingo English Test	115+

Comprehensive Review

The University of California evaluates each prospective student holistically beyond just grades. By weighing academics, involvement in activities, and personal dimensions equally, admissions officers aim to build a diverse student body while upholding high academic standards.

> Applicants are assessed holistically based on 13 criteria

The UC evaluates first-year applicants based on a comprehensive set of thirteen different criteria to assess an applicant's academic achievements and their potential contributions to the intellectual life at a UC campus[68]. The key components include the student's course rigor, grades in the A-G subjects, extracurricular activities, and responses to four short essays. These 'personal insight questions' allow applicants to provide context about their unique experiences, achievements, and aspirations and explain how they have shaped them as a person.

Students are responsible for accurately self-reporting their academic records and grades from the transcript. Any inconsistencies between self-reported and official transcripts after admission may lead to a rescinded offer. With the

> UC applications include the transcript, GPA, four short essays, and extracurriculars

exception of UC Berkeley[69], the UC system does not accept or consider letters of recommendation[70] as part of the application review.

Students can apply to any of the nine undergraduate campuses through the UC App[71], an online platform designed explicitly for the UC system.

> Apply to nine campuses in the UC App between Oct 1 and Nov 30

Applicants enter their personal data, coursework, grades, personal insight questions, and extracurricular activities only once before selecting all desired UC campuses. The UC App opens annually on August 1 to review and prepare the application materials. The filing period runs from October 1 through November 30 each year.

If a student applies to multiple UC campuses, each location independently evaluates the application without knowledge of the applicant's status at other campuses[72]. For example, UC Santa Cruz's admissions office does not consider whether the applicant also applied to UC Irvine or was already accepted by UCLA. Each campus makes its admission decision independently based on the comprehensive review.

> Each location reviews applicants independently from other UC campuses

UC comprehensive review: 13 admissions criteria

1. Academic GPA in all completed A-G courses, with additional points for UC-certified honors courses
2. Number of, content, and performance in academic courses beyond the minimum A-G requirements
3. Number of and performance in UC-approved honors, AB, IB higher level, and transferable college courses
4. Being ranked in the top 9 percent of the high school class in junior year (California residents only)
5. Rigor of the senior-year program, including type and number of academic courses planned or in progress
6. Academic performance relative to educational opportunities available in the student's high school
7. Outstanding performance in one or more specific subject areas
8. Outstanding work in one or more special projects in any academic field

9. Recent improvement in academic performance as indicated by GPA and quality of coursework completed or in progress
10. Special talents, achievements, and awards in various fields such as visual and performing arts, communication or athletic endeavors, proficiency in other languages, unusual promise for leadership such as significant community service or significant participation in student government
11. Completing special projects within the high school curriculum or school projects
12. Academic accomplishments considering life experiences and special circumstances, including disabilities, low family income, first generation to attend college, need to work, refugee or veteran status
13. Location of high school and residence

You may have noticed that the UC evaluation criteria do *not* include standardized tests scores like the SAT or ACT. In 2021, the UC system implemented a test-blind policy. Under this policy, SAT or ACT scores are not considered for admission. In fact, the UC App no longer provides a field for submitting standardized test results. However, once a student is admitted, their exam scores may be used to receive credits for specific general education classes or to waive requirements.

Priority Admission for California Residents

As a public institution supported by California taxpayers, the University of California is committed to prioritizing in-state applicants in its admissions process. This is reflected in the increasing percentage of admitted California students, rising from 63% in 2021 to 68% in 2023[73].

Chapter 5— California's Three-Tier Model

In the same period, the admission rate for international students decreased from 15% to 13%. In 2023, the campuses with the highest acceptance rates for international students were UC Davis (22%), UC Irvine (20%), UC Santa Barbara (12%) and UC San Diego (12%). UC Berkeley and UC Merced had the lowest percentage at 7% each.

To further its mission of making higher education accessible for everyone, the University of California has two programs to ensure high-achieving California high school students secure spots.

The *Eligibility in the Local Context Program*[74] provides a 'bonus point' in the admissions process to students ranking in the top 9% of their California high school. In addition, ELC-eligible students denied from all campuses they applied to are offered a spot at another UC campus with available space. Through the *Statewide Admissions Guarantee*[75], students in the top 9% of all California high schools are guaranteed admission to at least one UC campus, typically Merced or Riverside.

> The top 9% of California high school students are guaranteed a spot at a UC campus

The UC admissions office automatically screens all applications and identifies applicants eligible for both programs based on the recalculated GPA and A-G courses, with no extra paperwork needed. After submitting their application, students can verify their placement within the top 9% by selecting the 'view how your application is reviewed' link in the UC App. Both programs help qualified California residents gain access to the world-class UC system.

Chapter 6 – The Admissions Process

By now, you might have noticed that the admissions process of American colleges differs from what you are used to in your home country. Even for American applicants, the landscape has shifted in recent years, making it unfamiliar territory for parents recalling their own experiences. To better understand the main drivers of the admissions process, let us break it down into its core components.

The Admissions Office

What happens once you hit the 'submit' button of the online application? Who reviews your application? How does a college determine whether to accept or reject you? Every college has a team of experts in charge of admissions. The admissions office evaluates all applications, selects the incoming class, and oversees enrollment. In essence, these professionals are the gatekeepers of college admissions. Before exploring strategies to navigate the admissions process, let us examine the various roles in the admissions office.

> The admissions office decides on acceptances and rejections

As head of the organization, the Director of Admissions oversees all admissions strategies, operations, and personnel. The director formulates policies, objectives, and procedures that align with the

Chapter 6 – The Admissions Process

overarching institutional goals and enrollment strategies. These objectives, for instance, may include increasing diversity by admitting students from underrepresented communities, upholding academic standards by selecting high-performing applicants, or expanding the college's reach by attracting more international students. Goals vary across colleges and can change annually.

The outreach and recruitment team organizes recruitment events, markets the college to prospective students, and builds relationships with representatives of high schools and community colleges. Institutions with many applicants from abroad have international admissions specialists. While a separate office typically manages financial assistance, the financial aid liaison within the admissions office collaborates closely with them.

> The admissions office shapes the incoming class to reflect the institutional goals

Admissions officers are on the front lines of the college application process; they directly engage with prospective students and are the first to read and evaluate applications. Typically, admissions officers specialize in specific geographic territories, allowing them to familiarize themselves with the unique characteristics of their assigned area. Through this specialization, they can evaluate applicants in the context of locally available opportunities. Assigned regions can range from several U.S. states to a single school district, depending on the size of the applicant pool from that area. Further, admissions officers represent the college at recruitment events and may conduct interviews with applicants during the admissions cycle.

> Admissions officers are specialized by geographical areas

Competitive institutions receiving tens of thousands of applications may hire temporary staff to assist with reading and pre-screening the high volume of applications. Admissions officers often work in pairs to reduce potential bias, and many colleges pair newly recruited officers with more experienced ones. Junior officers are often recent college graduates who previously worked as student tour guides or part-time in the admissions office. The paired officers may independently assess the entire application or divide the different components like academics, extracurriculars, essays, etc. Regardless of the specific approach, most admissions offices follow standard practices in rendering admissions decisions. Let us have a look at them.

> Admissions officers review applications as a team or individually

How does the Evaluation Process Work?

The overarching goal of the admissions office is to determine how to achieve optimal enrollment by balancing the characteristics of the incoming class – while maintaining the college's financial stability. This evaluation process is called 'shaping the class' and assesses how individual applicants fit into the larger picture of the incoming class. While details and terminology can differ, most colleges use a collaborative model and follow standard protocols in their admissions process. This collaborative approach begins with an initial assessment by the assigned regional admissions officer and ends with the admissions committee deciding whether a

> The admissions committee decides which applicants are admitted

Chapter 6 – The Admissions Process

student is accepted or rejected. These committees, which usually include several regional admissions officers, the Head of Admissions, and sometimes even faculty members or other university staff, play a pivotal role in shaping the incoming class – their decisions directly impact the future of the college community.

> -Likely to admit
> -Toss-up
> -Likely to reject
> -Reject

As colleges strive to get a balanced freshman class based on institutional priorities, applications undergo a thorough review. Most admissions teams use a categorization system to move applications through multiple review cycles. While the terminology may differ, the primary categories usually include tags such as 'likely to be admitted' (sometimes called 'shoo-in application'), 'possibly admit' or 'toss-up,' 'likely to be rejected,' and 'almost certain to be rejected.'

In the first step, the assigned regional officer conducts the initial review of an application. This officer, who is familiar with the local context and the college's specific requirements, verifies the applicant's academic qualifications. Large colleges with a high volume of applications may rely on automatic algorithms for the initial screening. Some colleges combine a student's GPA and standardized test scores into one composite number, the academic index. If an applicant's grades and test scores do not meet the school's minimum expectations, the application is very likely to be marked for rejection.

> A regional officer or automatic algorithm screens the academics

While excellent academics are essential, good grades and test scores alone will not get you into a highly selective college; yet without them, your application is unlikely to make it to the next stage, the holistic review performed by the admissions committee.

Once an application passes the initial academic scrutiny, the regional officer examines the qualitative parts of the application, such as essays, letters of recommendation, or extracurriculars. Based on the strength of the application, the officer assigns a category ranging from 'likely to be admitted' to 'almost certain to be rejected.' On average, admissions officers spend about eight minutes[76] per application, but keep in mind that this average includes the full range of applicants – those who clearly do not meet the academic minimum as well as extraordinary 'shoo-in' applicants who are easy admits. Admissions officers do not dedicate too much time to the straightforward decisions on either end of the spectrum, as they can be quickly identified and processed. Instead, they spend most of their time reviewing promising applicants in the middle range, whose admission likelihood depends on how they compare against other competitive candidates. These applications warrant extensive consideration of all elements – academics, extracurricular activities, letters of recommendation, and essays.

> The academic index needs to meet the minimum to move on to holistic evaluation

> Admissions officers evaluate and suggest candidates to the committee

Following the initial evaluation, the application advances to the next phase, the comprehensive review performed by the admissions committee. During committee meetings, admissions officers introduce qualified applicants from their region. Regional officers advocate for their candidates' admission by highlighting why they believe these applicants are a good fit.

Decisions on acceptances are typically made collaboratively by the committee rather than individual officers. Throughout the lengthy review cycle, applications are often reviewed multiple times. As this process is driven by institutional priorities and the goal of building a well-balanced class, it is not uncommon that an application moves from the admit to the reject pile (or vice versa), sometimes even multiple times. As most selective colleges have adopted holistic admissions, let us examine what this process entails in more detail.

> The admissions committee decides on acceptances, waitlists, & rejections

Holistic Review Beyond Academics

Competitive colleges could fill their incoming classes with qualified applicants many times over. For example, UCLA received over 173,000 applications[77] for its fall 2024 incoming class. Without a doubt, many of these applicants were highly qualified and would thrive if admitted. However, UCLA only has space for about 6,500 freshmen every year, forcing the admissions office to look beyond the GPA to identify its incoming class. This broader evaluation approach is known as holistic review.

Like the UCs, an increasing number of colleges evaluate their applicants by considering not only GPA and test scores but also extracurricular involvement, personal characteristics, demographics, and potential contributions to the campus community. Some experts estimate that quantitative elements like GPA, course rigor, and standardized tests account for about 50% of the admissions process. However, since each college has its own priorities, it is safe to assume that there is no fixed formula.

In addition to academics, colleges highly value personal qualities. They actively look for evidence of leadership, initiative, creativity, and dedication through club participation, sports, or community service. Admissions officers are particularly interested in students who exhibit resilience, curiosity, and a willingness to engage with diverse perspectives. An applicant's personality, values, and aspirations can shine through in their essays, letters of recommendation, and, in some cases, interviews. This emphasis on personal qualities underscores the unique value each applicant brings to the table.

> Holistic evaluation = academics, leadership, talents, demographics, personal qualities, and potential contributions

By considering a wide range of factors, admissions officers aim to identify individuals who will thrive academically and contribute positively to the campus community. To facilitate this comprehensive assessment, colleges can apply various categorization systems to score their applicants. They utilize detailed rubrics to evaluate candidates across multiple rating criteria and scoring scales. For example, the University of Washington assigns numerical ratings on a scale of 1 to 9

Chapter 6 – The Admissions Process

to each applicant across academics, personal qualities, and overall application strength. The University of Michigan[78] employs a 5-point scale ranging from 'outstanding' to 'below average/poor,' while the University of California rates on thirteen specific factors[79].

The holistic review process benefits colleges more than applicants. Admission officers have more flexibility in assessing applicants, allowing them to create a diverse and well-rounded student body aligned with the institution's values and goals – gaining them points in college rankings. However, it also introduces subjectivity and lack of transparency into the admissions process. As a result, the admissions process and its outcomes have become unpredictable for applicants. A student admitted to the class of 2024 may have been rejected the year before.

> Holistic review is opaque, dynamic, and unpredictable

Critics of holistic review point out the risk of the process being biased and lacking transparency. The subjective nature of holistic assessment means that admissions decisions may be influenced by factors that are difficult to quantify or objectively measure. The lack of transparency can make the admissions process unpredictable and can feel unfair to applicants. While they got rejected, their friend with a lower GPA was admitted. It is easy to compare GPAs but difficult to objectively gauge the qualitative elements of an application – be it your own or the profile of other candidates. The additional focus on extracurricular activities, personal essays, and other non-academic factors places significant pressure on teenagers to excel both in and out of school. The running joke about having to win the Nobel Prize or cure cancer to get admitted to highly selective colleges may be exaggerated; nevertheless, holistic review significantly increases the stress and anxiety experienced by applicants and their families.

Admission Plans

Unless they take a gap year, American teenagers apply to colleges before they graduate high school. Depending on the admission plan they select, students submit their applications in the fall or winter of their senior year. Amidst the thousands of colleges to choose from, there are also various admission plans to navigate. Each college operates under its own set of rules and application periods, ranging from legally binding applications to admitting students as they apply. Understanding decision deadlines for every admission plan is crucial, as colleges will not accept applications once the submission deadline has passed! Keep in mind that all application deadlines are in the local time zone of the respective college, rather than your own. Since each option presents unique benefits and drawbacks, let us have a closer look at the various plans.

> Students apply to colleges before they graduate from high school

Regular Decision

Most students choose the standard admission plan, known as regular decision. This option allows them to apply to multiple colleges without any strings attached. Regular decision deadlines vary by

> Common deadlines are Nov 30, Jan 1, Feb 1, and Feb 15

institution but typically fall between early January and mid-February. The exception to this general rule is the University of California, which has its application deadline on November 30. This outlier serves as a reminder that it is absolutely critical to double-check all submission deadlines! Maintaining a spreadsheet that tracks all deadlines ensures you do not miss one.

Regular decision offers the advantage of more preparation time for your applications and the freedom to compare multiple college offers. RD deadlines extend until the winter of the senior year, giving students more time to perfect their essays and gather all necessary materials like letters of recommendation. Applying RD also allows students to include the first quarter or semester grades of their senior year, which can be a GPA boost if they improved their academic performance. Since RD decisions are non-binding, admitted students have until May 1 to compare financial aid packages, revisit campuses, and make a final decision. This way, students and their families can make a more informed decision.

> Most applicants apply to the regular decision pool

While regular decision has benefits, it also presents challenges. As colleges typically communicate admissions decisions around March, applying RD can extend stress and uncertainty well into the spring of students' senior year. In addition, applicant pools are larger, making the selection process more competitive and rigorous. Receiving a college acceptance and financial aid offer later in the year also leaves less time for families to budget for college expenses.

> More time to prepare but also more competition

This can be particularly challenging for those relying on financial aid to fund their education. Some scholarships may prioritize early applicants or have deadlines that align more closely with early application timelines, potentially limiting opportunities for students applying in the regular decision cycle.

Early Admission Options

In efforts to expedite the admissions process, some colleges introduced admission plans allowing students to apply early. This way, they receive a decision before the regular decision cycle, usually by December. Early applications can benefit both students and colleges. Receiving a decision early can significantly alleviate stress for students. In addition, applicants can use the early application options to demonstrate their commitment to a particular college as their top choice, potentially increasing their chances of admission. On the other hand, students considering an early application need to get all their ducks in a row and have their essays, letters of recommendation, test scores, and (translated) transcripts ready before fall – there is no point in applying early if you do not have a solid application to submit!

> Apply early for a faster decision

> Have your application ready by fall

Colleges have much to gain from early admission cycles. These programs allow them to secure a portion of their incoming class earlier, which aids in enrollment management. In addition, early application programs also enable colleges to identify and admit highly qualified candidates who are enthusiastic about attending their institution. Let us have a closer look at the three distinct ways to apply early to a college.

Early Decision

> Pick one (and only one!) college for early decision – ED is legally binding

The early decision plan allows students to apply and commit to their favorite college early. If admitted, the student makes a binding commitment to enroll at that institution and must withdraw all other applications. When applying early decision, be sure that this college is the right choice for you and that you can afford it, even without any merit aid. While they vary by school, ED deadlines typically fall between early and mid-November, and decisions are released in mid-December. Some colleges also offer a second ED round with a deadline in early January, allowing students rejected in ED1 to commit to their second-choice school.

> Common deadlines are Nov 1 or Nov 15 (ED1) and Jan 1 or Jan 15 (ED2)

Colleges benefit from the early decision plan beyond just identifying passionate applicants. It allows them to secure a portion of their incoming class from a pool of students who are guaranteed to attend. They can lock in a subset of their incoming class before the regular admissions cycle, easing uncertainty about yield rates later on. Since accepted students must attend unless they can prove a new financial hardship, ED is an effective tool for yield management, which can improve a college's status in college rankings.

> **ED helps with yield management**

In college admissions, 'yield' refers to the percentage of admitted students who choose to enroll at a particular college after receiving an acceptance letter. The yield rate reflects how competitive and attractive a college is in comparison to others. A high yield indicates that more admitted students chose to enroll. On the other hand, a lower yield rate signals that students value this institution less than other schools. While Harvard and Stanford have yield rates of 82%[80], other colleges have rates between 25% and 30%. Since they know that not all admitted students will attend, admissions offices must consider their previous yield rates and adjust the number of accepted students accordingly. You can compare this concept to an airline overbooking flights. As there is always a certain number of passengers not showing up for their flight, airlines sell more tickets than seats on the airplane to ensure that every seat is occupied when the plane takes off.

> **Yield management is like an airline overbooking flights**

However, admitting more students due to yield management makes a college look less selective, a key criterion in college rankings. ED helps colleges balance the factors influencing their yield, as it prohibits the admitted student from attending a different institution. Since early decision is legally binding, colleges can protect their yield rate by 'locking in' applicants early in the application cycle. While advantageous for colleges from a planning and yield management perspective, ED has drawn criticism for favoring wealthier applicants who can afford to pay the full tuition rate.

Applying through the ED program offers multiple benefits to students but also comes with some drawbacks. One of the advantages is that ED applicants receive a decision by December. Successful applicants do not have to work on additional applications, allowing them to focus on their schoolwork and save further application fees. The streamlined process of ED can alleviate the application fatigue many students experience. The most significant advantage, however, is that ED increases the odds of acceptance. Applying early signals to a college that it is the student's top choice, and they are ready to commit.

> ED has significantly higher acceptance rates

Consequently, many colleges report higher acceptance rates for early decision than for the regular cycle. For example, in 2023, Brown's ED acceptance rate was 12.9% compared to just 3.9% in the regular decision cycle, and Harvard accepted 7.6% of all ED applicants versus 2.3% from the regular decision pool[81]. Some colleges admit most of their incoming class from the ED pool. For instance, 60% of Boston University's incoming class of 2028 will come from their two rounds of early decision[82], leaving less than half of the spots for applicants from the regular decision cycle. To obtain the most recent statistics for your colleges of interest, check their admissions websites and the Common Data Set for past admissions data.

While applying via early decision offers a statistical advantage in the admission process, it is not the right path for everyone. ED applicants commit to a college without being able to compare financial offers from other schools. If financial aid is a consideration, this can be a major drawback since you do not have the opportunity to compare aid packages.

In addition, colleges have no incentive to offer competitive merit scholarships in the ED cycle, as there is no risk of losing applicants to another college. Committing to a college through ED means you must be absolutely sure that this institution is the best fit for you – academically, socially, and financially. If you have doubts whether a college is right for you or want the flexibility to choose from multiple offers, ED is not your best option.

> With ED, you cannot compare offers from other colleges

Early Action and Restrictive Early Action

> Early action is not binding and allows other early applications

As colleges realized the advantages of shaping their incoming class earlier in the admissions cycle, some began offering early action plans. Early action is a non-binding option to apply early and receive an admissions decision ahead of the regular decision pool. EA allows students to apply to multiple colleges early in their senior year, while still having the flexibility to consider other offers before making a final decision. Most early action deadlines are set for November 1 or 15, and decisions are usually released mid-December. It bears repeating that it is critical to carefully check all application deadlines for each institution you are considering!

> Common EA deadlines are Nov 1, Nov 15, and Dec 1

Students applying through restrictive early action also submit their applications by an early deadline, usually in November, and receive their admissions decisions by December. Restrictive early action combines elements of EA and ED. Like early action, REA is non-binding but, like ED, restricts where else the student can apply. While REA allows students to apply to other colleges through the regular decision cycle, it typically restricts them from applying to other colleges in their EA, ED, or any other early application plans. Depending on the specific REA policies, a college may allow exceptions, such as applying early to public universities, international institutions, or colleges with rolling admissions. For example, Stanford's REA policy allows early non-binding applications to public institutions like the EA program of the University of North Carolina at Chapel Hill and non-binding applications to colleges that require an early application to be considered for merit scholarships, such as the University of Southern California[83]. REA can be a strategic choice for students who have a clear first-choice college and are looking for an early response without the binding commitment of ED. However, students need to carefully weigh these benefits against the limitations of applying early to other institutions.

> Common REA deadlines are Nov 1 and Nov 15

> REA is non-binding but limits other early applications

Comparison of common application plans:

	ED	EA	REA	RD
Limited?	yes: 1 ED only	no: unlimited EA	yes: 1 REA only, no ED, some exceptions for EA	no
Legally binding?	yes	no	no	no
Allows other early applications?	yes: EA allowed, but must be withdrawn if admitted	yes: multiple EA and 1 ED allowed	no (some exceptions)	yes
Allows RD applications?	yes: must be withdrawn if admitted in ED	yes	yes	yes
Compare financial aid packages?	no	yes	yes	yes

Rolling Admissions

Some colleges review applications on a continuous basis, a practice referred to as rolling admissions. Students can apply during an application window that usually starts in August or September and lasts through the spring. Admissions officers evaluate applications as they are received and offer admission until all spots in the incoming class are filled. Applicants may receive their decision within a few weeks of submission.

Rolling admissions admits students on an ongoing basis

Rolling admissions can be particularly advantageous for students who decide late in their senior year to apply to college or those who were not accepted to their initial choice and are seeking alternatives. Although rolling admissions accept applications over an extended period, they evaluate and accept students on an ongoing basis; consequently, those applying later in the cycle may encounter stiffer competition for the few remaining spots. In addition, financial aid and housing options may become more limited as time goes on. Students applying early in the process may have an advantage in securing both.

> Applying early increases your chances of admission & scholarships

Auto-Admit and Direct Admissions Programs

> Auto-admit programs guarantee admission for certain applicant profiles

Auto-admit programs, sometimes also called guaranteed admission, offer a streamlined path to admission for students meeting predefined criteria like having a minimum GPA or standardized test score. These programs are prevalent in public institutions and simplify the admissions process for high-achieving students and the admissions office. For instance, Arizona State University automatically admits non-resident applicants if their GPA in specific core subjects is at least 3.0. Alternatively, ASU also automatically admits students with an ACT score of 24 or higher or a minimum SAT score of 1180[84]. Many auto-admit programs benefit in-state applicants as part of the state's effort to retain their top students. Many public universities offer resident guarantees similar to the UC's admission guarantee for the top 9% of California high school students. Auto-admit programs encourage students to apply to a college, as they make the admission process more transparent and predictable. The decision to apply may be a 'no-brainer' for students who meet the criteria, as they provide a valuable safety net in the highly unpredictable college admissions process.

> The *Direct Admissions Program* encourages first-generation and low-income applicants

Traditionally, students must actively submit an application to benefit from an auto-admit program. However, the Common App recently launched its *Direct Admissions Program*[85] to increase the number of low-income and first-generation college students. Eligible students who have entered their personal information in the Common App are offered admission by one of the 70 participating colleges, even before submitting an application. This reverse admissions model aims to break the fear of rejection that often prevents underprivileged students from applying in the first place. Knowing they have a guaranteed spot when they apply encourages students to pursue a college education. While this program is currently only available to U.S. students, it is an initiative worth mentioning.

Regardless of the admission cycle or program you choose, it is essential to start working on your application as early as possible. Do not wait until you get close to the deadline. College applications require a lot of detailed information, and you can expect to draft, revise, and fine-tune your essays over weeks and months.

> Begin working on your applications as early as possible

Chapter 6 – The Admissions Process

Before we unpack what elements go into your application, let us look at the various online systems colleges use to receive and process applications.

Application Platforms

Most colleges offer two ways to apply: directly on their website or through a shared online platform. Applying directly on the college website requires students to fill in their information for each college separately. Using a shared platform saves time because applicants can enter most of their information just once and apply to several schools with the click of a button.

The Common App

What is today the gold standard for admissions platforms started in 1975 as a streamlining initiative by fifteen college admissions teams. After being paper based for three decades, the digital version of the Common App revolutionized the college application process. Allowing students to fill out a single application and submit it to multiple colleges with the click of a button made the admissions process much more efficient. For better or worse, without the online version of the Common App, the surge in applications over the past 20 years would not have been possible.

> The digital version of the *Common App* facilitated the surge of applications

Today, the Common App empowers over one million first-year and transfer students to apply to over 1,000 colleges each year. It is a one-stop solution for managing all your application materials, such as transcripts, standardized test scores, parental information, activity lists, and letters of recommendation, in one place. You only need to enter general data once, and you can add any school-specific material as needed.

> Apply to over 1,000 colleges

Thanks to its streamlined process, the Common App has enabled students to apply to more colleges than previous generations. Still, the Common App caps the number of colleges students can apply to at twenty. This limit usually suffices, but workarounds are available if you want to apply to more colleges. One method involves removing a college from your list after applying, which opens a new slot for an additional institution. Another approach is to set up a second Common App account with a different email address. As a third option, students can apply directly on the websites of any additional colleges but will need to enter all the application data manually. Nevertheless, applying to an excessive number of schools can be detrimental, as you may spread your efforts too thin, potentially compromising the quality of your applications.

> The *Common App* limits the number of applications to 20

The Common App is not just a platform to apply to colleges efficiently, but also a comprehensive resource for applicants. It provides detailed information on participating colleges, the specifics of the application process, and financial aspects. Use the 'Profile' tab to enter personal information like demographics, test scores, grades, family background, and personal statement. The 'Financial Aid' tab outlines various ways to pay for college expenses, including scholarships, loans, or work-study opportunities. In the 'College Search' tab, you can search for and add potential schools to your list. Once you add a college of interest, the Common App displays application details, such as deadlines, fees, and required material. In this section, you can also enter any college-specific documents, like supplemental essays. Use the 'Dashboard' tab to monitor your application progress by institution.

Create your *Common App* account anytime

Do not wait until senior year to set up your Common App account; there is no downside to creating it ahead of time. This way, you can familiarize yourself with the required data and material and be ready to start your applications when the time comes. While the Common App refreshes every year on August 1, all previously entered personal data will roll over[86]. Remember to check for any changes after account rollover, particularly whether there are new essay prompts or supplemental questions for the new application cycle. You do not want to end up working on last year's prompts and waste precious time. Once you submit your application in the Common App, you can no longer change any part of it – double-check every detail before hitting that 'submit' button! For more details about the Common App and how to fill it out, have a look at its comprehensive online application guide[87].

Verify the essay prompts after August 1

SCOIR

SCOIR, previously known as Coalition Application, is a platform designed to promote college access, particularly for lower income, underrepresented, and first-generation college students. Like the Common App, SCOIR allows students to research colleges, compile a portfolio of their work, and apply to member institutions. The platform also provides students with tools like virtual events sharing insights about participating colleges, help finding one's best fit, and the application process. SCOIR provides many resources and tutorials to help students craft compelling college essays and prepare for interviews. As of November 2023, 142 U.S. colleges accept applications through SCOIR.

Apply to over 140 member colleges

The UC and CSU Apps

California's two public university systems, the University of California and California State University, have developed their own online application platforms tailored to their unique admissions processes.

UC App

Students applying to any of the nine undergraduate UC campuses use the UC App[88]. This centralized portal allows applicants to enter their personal and academic details, self-report their coursework and grades, and respond to four short essay prompts. Standardized test

Use the UC App to apply to nine UC campuses at once

scores are not required, nor are letters of recommendation for most UC campuses. While students can create an account anytime, the application window for first-year applicants is between October 1 and November 30.

CalState Apply

The 23 campuses of the CSU system utilize a separate online application called CalState Apply[89]. This straightforward application focuses primarily on academic achievements without requiring essays or letters of recommendation. While there are set priority windows to apply, some CSU campuses may accept applications after the deadlines if space permits.

Apply to 23 CSUs through *CalState Apply*

The CSU offers multiple application windows throughout the academic year[90] for different entry terms. The most common application timeframe is for the fall quarter/semester, which can be submitted between October 1 and November 30. As fall marks the beginning of the academic year, this period is the most popular one, and students are encouraged to apply during this window to maximize their chances of admissions. Winter quarter admissions (June 1 to June 30) are less common, and not all CSU campuses offer a winter intake. Spring admissions (August 1 to 31) are available at many CSU campuses. They offer an alternative entry point for students who prefer to start college in the middle of the academic year. Summer admissions are typically geared toward specific programs and may not be widely available for all undergraduate majors. Like California, other U.S. states

Apply to CSUs multiple times per year

utilize centralized portals tailored to their public university systems, such as 'applyTexas'[91] for Texas institutions and 'applySUNY'[92] for those in New York State.

School-specific Applications

Most private colleges accept both the Common App and applications sent directly through their websites, but a handful of institutions mandate the use of their own application portals. The Massachusetts Institute of Technology[93] is the most prominent college not accepting the Common App. Instead, MIT uses its proprietary system designed for its specific, STEM-focused application process. Georgetown University[94] is the second private institution utilizing its own application system rather than the Common App.

Apply directly on the college website

Military academies like West Point[95] and the United States Naval Academy[96] also have their proprietary systems that assess applicants' potential for leadership, physical fitness, and commitment to service. At West Point, up to sixty international students are recruited every year. With these few exceptions in mind, it is generally best to use the Common App platform whenever possible, as it saves a lot of time when applying to more than one school.

College-Specific Portals

While submitting an application may feel like the last step in a long process, your journey is not over yet! After receiving an application

Chapter 6 – The Admissions Process

through the Common App or SCOIR, most colleges send an email asking applicants to create an account for their proprietary online portal. These portals are often the first place where updates and application decisions are posted. In addition, a college may use its portal to invite a student to an interview, request additional documents, or communicate deadlines for financial aid or housing.

Most colleges require you to set up an additional account on their portal

After submitting your application in the Common App, check your email account for an invitation to the college portal and set up your account as soon as possible. Remember to check your spam folder if you have not received an email invitation after a few days. Once activated, make it a habit to check your portals regularly, at least once a week, and more frequently as decision dates approach. Many colleges will not send email notifications to inform applicants of a change in the portal. Keep track of your login credentials in a secure, accessible location. If a college requests additional information or documents through the portal, respond promptly to avoid delays in your application review.

Regularly check all college portals for updates

Possible Application Outcomes

Most colleges pledge to send admissions decisions by April 1 to allow students enough time to consider their options before committing to a college by May 1. Applicants may receive various decisions from colleges to which they applied: being accepted, rejected, deferred, or waitlisted.

> Accepted: Congrats!
> Rejected: Don't take it personally!
> Deferred: 2nd chance with the regular pool
> Waitlisted: Maybe, maybe not

Being Admitted

Receiving an acceptance letter in your email or the college portal is the ideal outcome, as it means the college is offering admission for the upcoming academic term, usually starting in the fall. The acceptance will outline the next steps for enrollment, financial aid, and confirming your spot. Many colleges host 'admitted students days,' special open houses to convince accepted students to enroll. Even if you have toured the campus before, consider attending, as being admitted may change your perspective and priorities. Housing, on-campus food options, or access to the nearest airport may become more relevant than you previously thought. Reach out to faculty and current students to gather first-hand insights into academics and campus life. If financially feasible, visit or revisit the campuses after admission, at least the ones you are seriously considering.

> Attend 'admitted students day' to (re-)confirm that a college is a good fit

Some highly selective colleges send out 'likely letters' signaling to highly desirable applicants that they are strongly favored for admissions. These letters are sent before formal acceptances are released. They can create a win-win situation, allowing the college to secure their top prospects while giving applicants early peace of mind. Colleges may even include invitations to special events, such as an all-expenses paid campus visit. Occasionally, they go one step further and mail 'early writes,' which are early acceptance letters sent to their most appealing applicants.

> Likely letters and early writes lock in candidates before official acceptances

Once admissions decisions are officially released, the power shifts from the college to the applicants since they now choose and commit to their preferred institution. Receiving an acceptance letter is the outcome every applicant hopes for. As an admitted student, the next steps are straightforward – you pick your favorite college, if admitted to more than one, and commit by May 1.

Acceptance checklist:

- [ ] Visit all colleges you are seriously considering
- [ ] Accept the offer (= statement of intent to register) in the portal *before May 1*
- [ ] Submit the deposit
- [ ] Complete and return any required forms
- [ ] Apply for on-campus housing
- [ ] Finalize your financial aid and scholarship arrangements
- [ ] Submit final transcripts and standardized test scores
- [ ] Complete orientation modules and register for classes

- ☐ Sign up for health insurance via the college's plan or a private provider
- ☐ Apply for a F-1 student visa (international students)
- ☐ Attend admitted students day (recommended)
- ☐ Notify other colleges that you will not attend (optional)

Being Rejected

The other clear-cut decision in admissions is being rejected. While disappointing, rejections are an inevitable part of the college admissions process, and applicants should not take it as a reflection of their worth or abilities. Many colleges are inundated with tens of thousands of applications for a limited number of spots, making it impossible to admit all qualified applicants.

> Rejections are a natural part of college admissions

If you have new, compelling information not originally included in your application or believe your application was processed with an error, you could consider appealing the admissions decision. However, the chances of having a rejection overturned through an appeal are slim at best. Given the competitive nature of U.S. college admissions and the high likelihood of facing rejections, applying to a diverse range of institutions is essential. Cast a wide net to create a balanced list of reach, target, and safety schools. Rejected applicants will need to explore other academic options, such as attending a different college or reapplying in the future.

Acceptances and rejections are the clear-cut outcomes in college admissions, providing a definite answer and a straightforward path to

Chapter 6 – The Admissions Process

follow. The other potential outcomes, being deferred or waitlisted, are more complex, prolong a student's uncertainty, and require a higher degree of application management.

Being Deferred

Students applying in the early action or early decision cycle may be neither accepted nor rejected but receive a deferral. Being deferred means the college postpones a final decision until a later review round, usually regular decision. The admissions team sees promise in the deferred applicant but needs more time or information to decide. Perhaps the admissions office wants to reevaluate the candidate in the context of a larger applicant pool, or they want to see additional grades before finalizing their selections.

> Moved from early application to the regular decision pool

While a deferral can be disappointing, it also provides an opportunity to strengthen one's application and demonstrate continued interest. The admissions offices usually provide instructions on how to proceed and what additional material they may accept. Typically, the first step is to express continued interest by submitting a form or responding to an email. Colleges often ask applicants to submit a 'letter of continued interest,' a formal communication from the student expressing

> Write a LoCI and strengthen your profile

their continued interest in the institution. In this letter, students can reiterate their enthusiasm for the school, provide updates on achievements or activities, and emphasize why they are a good fit for the institution.

Some colleges allow deferred applicants to submit additional material, including updated grades, new awards or honors, improved test scores, or additional letters of recommendation. Reviewing the college's deferral policy and guidelines for submitting supplemental materials is essential; only provide additional material if the college asks for it. Other ways to show continued interest are attending (virtual) events or connecting with current students or alumni. Demonstrating your ongoing enthusiasm for the institution can positively impact the admissions decision. Since colleges often consider senior year grades in the regular admissions process, it is essential to maintain strong grades in 12th grade.

Nevertheless, being deferred to the regular decision cycle means your application is assessed within a much larger pool of applicants. Most colleges do not earmark or tag deferred applications, so admissions officers do not know that you applied in an earlier round. Your chances of being admitted are as high – or low – as for any other applicant in the regular decision cycle. While waiting for the outcome of the deferral, students should focus on completing any remaining applications for additional colleges of interest. It is essential to cast a wide net and keep one's options open, as a deferred application might not turn into an acceptance later.

> Continue to work on your other applications

Being Waitlisted

The second outcome that brings a lot of ambiguity is being waitlisted. In this case, an applicant is not admitted but placed on a waitlist, with the possibility of admission if spots become available later. Some colleges use the waitlist as a form of 'soft rejection' to let down an applicant more gently.

Other colleges use waitlists as holding grounds for qualified candidates and pull students from the list as they fill up and round off their incoming classes. Being waitlisted can be emotionally challenging, as students are in a state of limbo, unsure whether they will eventually be admitted. Like in a deferral, waitlisted applicants are asked to confirm their interest in remaining on the waitlist. Colleges usually provide specific instructions on how to stay on the waitlist and any additional materials being accepted. You can apply the strategies outlined for deferred students to strengthen your application.

> Waitlisted applicants may be considered if space opens up

The term waitlist is a misnomer as it conjures the image of a waitlist at a popular restaurant. Colleges usually do not have a numbered waitlist that admits students in order. Instead, they use the waitlist strategically to further shape their incoming class with a diverse student population based on their institutional needs. They may still need one more oboe player for their orchestra or a student from an underrepresented geographic area. Suppose an admitted

> Colleges use the waitlist to shape the incoming class

student majoring in marine biology who plays volleyball declines their offered spot. Chances are that the admissions team will offer admission to a waitlisted applicant with a similar profile.

As these priorities and considerations are not transparent to the applicants, the best a student can do is continue to show interest while considering their other options. Some colleges admit hundreds of waitlisted applicants, whereas others admit close to none. To gauge your odds of coming off the waitlist at a particular college, check their Common Data Set. For example, in 2023, Stanford University admitted 76 students out of 607 waitlisted applicants[97]. Waitlist results can be released anytime from May through August.

> Love the school that loves you

With the outcome of the waitlist uncertain, it is critical to commit to a different college by the May 1 deadline. You commit by accepting their offer in the designated portal and paying the enrollment deposit. Should you gain admission from the waitlisted institution later, you can withdraw your prior commitment and commit to the previously waitlisted college.

> Don't rely on the waitlist. Commit to a different college by May 1!

However, this may result in a penalty payment or forfeiture of the original deposit. Additionally, if you have already paid tuition or housing fees to the first college, you may not be eligible for a full refund, and there may be additional penalties associated with canceling housing contracts or meal plans. If you want to withdraw your commitment to the first college in favor of the previously waitlisted one, you must notify the admissions offices as soon as possible. Colleges generally understand the challenging decisions you face and often are willing to assist in mitigating any financial repercussions.

Application Fees

Most colleges charge a fee when students apply, typically ranging from $50 to $90 per institution. These fees help cover costs like staffing and maintaining online application platforms. Some schools charge slightly higher fees for international applicants to account for additional administrative costs associated with processing foreign credentials and documents. For example, the fee to apply to the University of California is $80 for domestic applicants and $95 for international students[98]. The application fee is applied per campus, so a student applying to five UC locations would pay $400 as a domestic applicant and $475 as an international student.

Application fees range from $50 to $95

Paying application fees is straightforward. The most common option is to submit payment by credit card through the application portal or Common App. Some colleges also accept checks and money orders, which require mailing the payment, so you need to consider additional time for postal delivery to meet application deadlines. International students may use a credit

Pay fees by credit card, check, money order, Western Union, or Flywire

card or international money transfer services like Western Union or Flywire.

Keep track of application deadlines and acceptable payment methods for each prospective college to ensure you have the necessary funds in your account and complete payments on time. International applicants should account for currency conversion or transaction fees.

Since application fees can accumulate quickly when applying to multiple campuses, many colleges offer fee waivers for students demonstrating financial need. Eligibility may be based on qualifying for programs like free/reduced school lunch, public assistance, the College Board SAT fee waiver program, or federal TRIO initiatives[99]. International students may be eligible for fee waivers, but availability and criteria can differ from those for domestic applicants.

Check if you are eligible for a fee waiver

Chapter 7 – Qualitative Components of an Application

While college admissions in some countries rely solely on academic performance in high school or university entrance exams, U.S. institutions adopt a more comprehensive approach. Academics remain the foundation, but American colleges evaluate applicants across multiple dimensions. Students submit qualitative documents that offer a glimpse into their unique experiences, personal attributes, and aspirations. This chapter explores the qualitative components of a college application.

Quantitative elements:

→ **GPA** is critical for evaluating an applicant's classroom performance
→ **Standardized test scores** provide a nationally standardized benchmark of academic skills and college readiness

Qualitative elements:

→ **Essays** showcase applicants' storytelling abilities and are a window into their mindset, values, and potential contributions
→ **Letters of recommendation** from teachers, counselors, or other mentors provide outside perspectives evaluating the applicant's intellect, character strengths, and leadership potential

→ **Extracurricular activities** demonstrate time management skills and commitment outside the classroom
→ **Competitions and awards** showcase an applicant's achievements within academic or extracurricular domains
→ **Interviews** (where offered) allow the applicant to articulate their motivations directly to the admissions officer
→ **Supplemental submissions** like portfolios, videos, or auditions showcase exceptional talents in areas like art, music, theater, dance, or other specialized skills relevant to intended programs of study
→ **Demonstrated interest** signals a preference for the institution

In holistic admissions, students present various documents illustrating their qualitative attributes alongside academic achievements. Each component is like a puzzle piece, providing additional information. All pieces together reveal the applicant as a multidimensional individual beyond grades and test scores. This allows admissions officers to evaluate the student from multiple vantage points.

While applicants are responsible for initiating, submitting, and overseeing their application in the Common App or another platform, some parts of the application must be managed and submitted by the school counselor.

Overview of shared responsibilities:

	Applicant	School Counselor
Personal Information	✓	
Academic transcripts	self-report	official transcript
Standardized tests	✓	
Essays	✓	

Chapter 7 – Qualitative Components of an Application

Extracurricular activities	✓	
Awards and competitions	✓	
Supplemental material	✓	
Financial aid applications	✓	
Invite LoR recommenders	✓	
Submit LoR		✓
School profile		✓
Application fees	✓	
Language proficiency (intl. only)	✓	
Visa application (intl. only)	✓	

Personal Information

When applying through the Common App or another portal, applicants must provide a range of personal data. This information serves a dual purpose as it facilitates the application processing and provides valuable context of each applicant. Applicants enter basic personal information like their name, birthday, address, citizenship, family information, language proficiency, and other demographic data.

-Personal data
-Demographics
-Courses
-Grades
-Standardized tests
-Financial data

They also self-report their academic history including GPA, past and planned high school courses, expected graduation date, and, if applicable, standardized test scores; their high school counselor submits the official transcript separately. Colleges may also ask for financial information like household income, with more details requested in the separate financial aid-specific forms like the FAFSA or CSS Profile.

College Essays

Most colleges ask applicants to submit at least one essay, allowing them to gain deeper insights into the applicant's unique experiences, challenges, and writing skills. Articulating one's thoughts in a structured manner is critical for academic success in college. Essays showcase an applicant's writing proficiency, including grammar, punctuation, and essay organization. Many prompts assess critical thinking, problem-solving skills, and creativity by analyzing how applicants respond to questions, structure arguments, or engage with complex topics.

> Essays give insights into writing skills, personal values, motivations, unique experiences, and local context

> Tell your story in your own voice to differentiate yourself from other applicants

In a competitive applicant pool full of students with stellar grades and test scores, essays offer the opportunity to stand out by highlighting personal experiences and perspectives. Some prompts specifically ask about the applicant's interest in the institution. These essays allow students to demonstrate their genuine enthusiasm by displaying detailed knowledge about the college and how its specific programs align with their academic interests and career goals. While time-consuming, essays allow applicants to present their personalities and unique perspectives, providing a more holistic view of who they are.

Each college tackles the enormous task of reading and assessing thousands of submitted essays in their own way. Some hire temporary readers to rate the essays before the official review in admissions, while others have the assigned officer read all material themselves. One can only speculate how one individual can evaluate thousands of essays during one admissions period.

Write strong first and last paragraphs

Considering the sheer volume of essays reviewed during one admissions period, putting extra effort into crafting the first and last paragraphs is recommended. The quality of these sections may determine whether the reader will read and examine the whole essay in detail. You can find many examples of personal statements online or purchase or rent books with college-specific essay collections. We will discuss strategies for essay writing in a dedicated chapter.

The Personal Statement

The main college essay, often called the personal statement, requires students to reflect on their life experiences, values, and goals. At the same time, students can demonstrate their ability to write concisely

Personal statement = 250 to 650 words

and coherently on a given topic. The Common App offers seven different prompts to choose from. These prompts may change for every admissions cycle but have remained the same in past years. Always double-check the up-to-date prompts before drafting your essay. There is also the possibility of adding an optional essay about the impact of COVID-19 on one's life.

Personal Statement prompts (2023):

→ Some students have a background, identity, interest, or talent that is so meaningful they believe their application would be incomplete without it. If this sounds like you, then please share your story.
→ The lessons we take from obstacles we encounter can be fundamental to later success. Recount a time when you faced a challenge, setback, or failure. How did it affect you, and what did you learn from the experience?
→ Reflect on a time when you questioned or challenged a belief or idea. What prompted your thinking? What was the outcome?
→ Reflect on something that someone has done for you that has made you happy or thankful in a surprising way. How has this gratitude affected or motivated you?
→ Discuss an accomplishment, event, or realization that sparked a period of personal growth and a new understanding of yourself or others.
→ Describe a topic, idea, or concept you find so engaging that it makes you lose all track of time. Why does it captivate you? What or who do you turn to when you want to learn more?
→ Share an essay on any topic of your choice. It can be one you've already written, one that responds to a different prompt, or one of your own design.

The Common App sets a minimum of 250 and a maximum of 650 words for the personal statement. Be careful to stay within this word count, as the system will cut off your essay if it exceeds 650 words. Read the prompt carefully and answer it completely. Remember, essays are not only a way to stand out, but they also show that you can follow instructions. Writing the essay is your first homework assignment from the college, and you want to put your best foot forward. Some colleges may also require supplemental essays or short questions in addition to the personal statement.

Personal Insight Questions

The University of California does not accept the personal statement. Instead, they use their own essay prompts, the so-called personal insight questions. Students must answer four out of eight questions with a maximum of 350 words each.

Up to 350 words for each Personal Insight Question

UC Personal Insight Questions prompts (2023):

→ Describe an example of your leadership experience in which you have positively influenced others, helped resolve disputes or contributed to group efforts over time.
→ Every person has a creative side, and it can be expressed in many ways: problem solving, original and innovative thinking, and artistically, to name a few. Describe how you express your creative side.
→ What would you say is your greatest talent or skill? How have you developed and demonstrated that talent over time?

→ Describe how you have taken advantage of a significant educational opportunity or worked to overcome an educational barrier you have faced.

→ Describe the most significant challenge you have faced and the steps you have taken to overcome this challenge. How has this challenge affected your academic achievement?

→ Think about an academic subject that inspires you. Describe how you have furthered this interest inside and/or outside of the classroom.

→ What have you done to make your school or your community a better place?

→ Beyond what has already been shared in your application, what do you believe makes you a strong candidate for admissions to the University of California?

Letters of Recommendation

Letters of recommendation are another unique element of the American admissions process. They add depth to an applicant's profile by offering third-party perspectives on their strengths, accomplishments, and personal qualities. In a competitive pool of applicants with similar academic credentials, compelling letters of recommendation can potentially tip the balance in favor of admission.

> Recommendations provide an outside perspective

Selecting Recommenders

In their letters, recommenders typically share anecdotes highlighting a student's work ethic, leadership, or community involvement — qualities

Chapter 7 – Qualitative Components of an Application

that transcripts and test scores cannot convey. Colleges typically prefer recommendations from junior-year teachers in core academic subjects, ideally aligned with the student's declared major. It may be a good idea to approach teachers from different academic fields, as this can provide diverse perspectives on your strengths.

Most colleges require two letters from subject teachers and one from the high school counselor. The counselor's letter can provide a broader context for the student's academics and role within the school community. Some colleges allow an additional letter from a non-academic recommender like a coach, mentor, or boss who can attest to the student's qualities or unique talents outside of school. When selecting recommenders, it is crucial to choose individuals who know you well and are likely to write strong, supportive letters. The quality of insight matters more than the recommender's title.

> 3 recommenders: 2 teachers & high school counselor

Approach potential recommenders well before application deadlines, ideally months beforehand, to give them ample time to write thoughtful letters. Many students may request letters from popular teachers, potentially forcing them to limit the number of letters they can write. When requesting a recommendation, ask the teacher whether they can write a positive letter. Provide them with a resume or summary of your academic achievements, personal traits, and specific strengths or anecdotes you would like them to address. This information, often called a 'brag sheet,'[100] can help them craft a more detailed and personalized recommendation. While mentioning the

> Ask teachers early if they can write a positive letter of recommendation

colleges and programs you plan to apply to may be helpful, emphasize that the recommenders should *not* include the name of any specific institution in the letter. Once uploaded, recommenders cannot make any changes, and you certainly do not want to apply to the University of Florida with a letter of recommendation referencing Texas A&M.

The Common App facilitates letters of recommendation by allowing you to invite your recommenders and emailing them a link to upload their letters. The Common App also requests additional information from the recommenders, such as the subject they taught you and their overall assessment of your academic performance. Remind your recommenders of upcoming deadlines, and always thank them for their time and effort.

Ensuring Credibility

> Waiving your FERPA rights enhances the credibility of your recommendations

The Family Educational Rights and Privacy Act is a federal law that gives students the right to view their educational records, including letters of recommendation. However, educational advisors recommend waiving one's FERPA rights as a standard practice to ensure the recommender's assessment is confidential and truthful. By waiving your rights, you significantly enhance the credibility of your recommenders and their letters, increasing their impact on the admissions process. In the Common App, waive your rights in the 'FERPA release authorization' under 'My Colleges' and 'Recommenders and FERPA.'

Chapter 7 – Qualitative Components of an Application

Cultural Considerations

Understanding America's social norm of avoiding negative aspects or criticism in letters of recommendation is crucial. American recommendations do not provide a balanced perspective but enthusiastically emphasize the positive qualities – an approach that may not be shared by all cultural backgrounds. International students may need to guide their recommenders on the expectations of American-style recommendations to ensure their letters meet U.S. standards.

> American recommendations are enthusiastic

Extracurricular Activities and Awards

To gain a 360-degree view of applicants, colleges also consider how they spend their time outside the classroom. Extracurricular activities like sports, clubs, or music provide a window into students' interests and pursuits. A balanced activity list on top of solid academics suggests effective time management skills and a strong work ethic. Extracurriculars can also be a way to stand out from other applicants by showcasing your unique talents or unusual experiences that bring diversity to a college campus.

> Demonstrate continuity and progression in your activities

The Importance of Time and Commitment

When is the best time to start an extracurricular activity? The time when you begin an activity can influence how admissions officers perceive it.

They may view an activity initiated shortly before college applications differently than a hobby a student has pursued for multiple years. Long-term commitment to an activity indicates persistence and the ability to stick with a task, qualities that admissions officers value.

> Time is a critical factor in turning a hobby into a passion project

Time is a critical factor in transforming a regular hobby into a 'passion project' or 'super-curricular' that sets an applicant apart. For instance, if a student dedicates five hours per week to an activity starting in their junior year, they can report 260 hours in their college application. However, the same weekly time commitment beginning at 9th grade results in 780 hours – a significant difference demonstrating sustained commitment! The longer you engage in an activity, the more likely you can demonstrate mastery, assume leadership positions, and use your experiences as a topic in your essays (two birds with one stone, so to speak).

Quality over Quantity

While sports and music immediately come to mind, many other areas can and should be considered. Internships and part-time jobs show initiative and real-world skills, while student council roles imply leadership and a commitment to school affairs. Joining debate or robotic clubs can demonstrate intellectual curiosity, and volunteering at a local food bank reflects social responsibility. Students in orchestras or theater productions can illustrate their creativity and communication skills. Applicants can also include significant family responsibilities such as caring for younger siblings or older family members.

Whatever they may be, students should participate in activities that hold personal meaning rather than just to enhance their college applications. Genuine enthusiasm shines through in the application, and admissions officers have developed a sense for identifying shallow or placeholder activities. Depth and commitment are more impressive than a long list of superficial involvements.

> Depth & commitment trump multiple superficial activities

Effectively Showcasing Extracurriculars

The Common App and the UC App provide limited space to describe extracurricular activities, requiring concise writing to convey meaningful and measurable information effectively. Keep a log of the time you dedicated to each activity, as the Common App asks to quantify the number of hours spent per week and year since 9th grade. List up to ten activities in the order of significance and, where possible, quantify your achievements (e.g., funds raised, people reached, awards won) to provide concrete evidence of your impact.

> List activities and awards in the order of significance

In the Common App, students have only 300 characters to describe each activity, meaning they have 50 to 70 words to detail the organization, their role, and the activity's scope. Use bulleted formatting to save space but avoid acronyms. At the same time, use the maximum number of words allowed to provide more details on roles and contributions.

Employ active, specific verbs, and include any skills that you learned. You may have guessed it from the wording of the field

MISSION: ACCEPTED!

'Position/Leadership description': admissions officers are looking for evidence of leadership experience– keep that in mind when describing your role and responsibilities in an activity. Using the full character limit can elevate a lackluster description into a compelling portrayal of your involvement in an activity. To illustrate this, let us compare the impact of the following two descriptions of the same activity.

	Example 1	Example 2
Activity type	Music: Vocal	Music: Vocal
Position / Leadership description (max. 50 characters)	Choir member (12 characters)	Soprano section leader and assistant choir leader (49 characters)
Organization (max. 100 characters)	Polyphonic Pioneers (19 characters)	Polyphonic Pioneers: audition-based show choir, nationally ranked, national and global performances (99 characters)
Description of activity, including accomplishments and awards (max. 150 characters)	I sing in the school choir and help with performances (53 characters)	Provide guidance to soprano section, lead section & choir rehearsals, help organize competition participation, plan and execute travel for whole choir (150 characters)

In addition to ten activities, applicants can enter up to five academic honors and awards, specified by their level of recognition (school, state/regional, national, international). In the tab 'Education,' include your awards, such as being an AP or National Merit Scholar, and your recognitions from competitions like the International Science and Engineering Fair, Siemens Competition, or Math Olympiad. In addition, you can include awards given by your high school, such as valedictorian or being on your high school's Honor Roll.

> List 15 activities / awards in the Common App and 20 in the UC App

The Common App separates activities and honors/awards into two separate sections. In contrast, the UC App consolidates these elements and provides 20 fields for extracurriculars, academic awards and honors, educational preparation programs, paid work experience, unpaid volunteering, and community service initiatives. The UC App also sets a word limit for each activity, giving you up to 350 characters, approximately 50 to 85 words, to highlight your accomplishments. Therefore, you can also apply the concise writing techniques recommended for the Common App's activity list to the UC application.

Interviews

Some colleges allow applicants to directly engage with college representatives or alumni. These interviews, which can occur in person or through video calls, provide a unique chance for applicants to share additional information about themselves and ask questions about the

> Interviews with admissions officers or alumni may be required or optional

institution. In the interview, students can showcase their personality, communication skills, and enthusiasm for the college. While some schools require interviews as a standard part of their application process, others offer the option to request one. Remember to take advantage of all optional opportunities presented during college admissions! Even if you feel intimidated, do not pass up the chance to strengthen your profile and demonstrate your genuine interest in attending.

The interview transforms an applicant from a statistic to an actual person. Schedule interviews as early as possible, as slots can fill quickly, especially for popular colleges or during peak application season. Before the meeting, thoroughly research the college's programs and culture and reflect on what makes it a good fit for you. Be prepared to discuss why you want to attend. Review your application and be familiar with what you have submitted, including your essays and activities.

> Schedule interviews as early as possible, as slots may be limited

Prepare answers for common interview questions such as

- → Tell me about yourself.
- → What are your academic or extracurricular interests?
- → What are your strengths and weaknesses?
- → Describe a project that you enjoyed.
- → Tell me about a challenge that you faced. (*Hint*: Focus on how you overcame the challenge and what you learned from it.)
- → Who is a role model in your life? Why?
- → What are you passionate about?
- → How will you contribute to our college community?
- → What do you do for fun?

Chapter 7 – Qualitative Components of an Application

It may also be helpful to prepare a list of thoughtful questions to ask the interviewer about the college programs, campus life, or their personal experiences at the college. You can practice for the interview with a family member or friend.

For the meeting, wear appropriate attire that shows you are taking it seriously. Arrive 15 minutes before an in-person interview or ensure your background is suitable for video calls. Video interviews may take place through software like Zoom[101] or admissions-specific applications like InitialView[102]. Occasionally, interviewers ask to pan the camera around to ensure you are alone in the room. Some colleges, like Claremont McKenna, record and file video interviews of international students. Most interviewers, however, submit a write-up of the conversation, which becomes part of the application file.

> Practice in a mock interview with a family member or friend

After the interview, send a thank-you email to your interviewer expressing your appreciation for their time and reiterate your interest in the college. While interviews can help in the holistic admissions process, they are just one component among many. An interview is as much an opportunity for you to learn more about the college as it is for the admissions team to get to know you better. Approach the interview as a conversation rather than an interrogation and use it to provide additional evidence for your enthusiasm for becoming part of their college community.

> Send a 'thank you' email after the interview

Videos

Like interviews, video submissions allow applicants to showcase their personalities in a dynamic format and connect with admissions committees on a more personal level. Brown, Tufts, the University of Chicago, and other colleges use supplemental videos as standard part of their admissions process. In some cases, colleges request a video submission when applicants are unable to schedule an interview. The supplemental video can be a self-produced video based on a selected prompt or a timed video statement responding to a randomly chosen question. For example, Swarthmore College[103] allows 30 seconds of preparation time and up to two takes before submitting the video response.

> Videos may be self-produced or a timed response to a randomly selected question

Your video should reflect who you are and illustrate your unique perspective. Ensure the video tells the admissions team something new about yourself; avoid repeating information already submitted in your application material.

> Be authentic and present something new about you

Creating a compelling video does not require expensive equipment – a smartphone and basic editing software are sufficient. Film in a well-lit area, ideally with natural light facing you to avoid shadows. Use a quiet room and consider an external microphone to ensure clear audio and a tripod or steady surface to prevent shaky footage. Use basic editing software like iMovie[104] to trim unnecessary parts, add text or transitions, and ensure the video meets the time requirement. Rehearse what you want to say to ensure you cover all your points succinctly. You can find many college application videos on YouTube to get a feel for what other applicants have submitted. However, it is important that your video is authentic and reflects your unique personality and narrative – do not just emulate what others have already done.

Supplemental Materials

Depending on the prospective college and major, students may be asked or required to submit additional materials, often referred to as 'supplementals.' These materials can include research papers, art portfolios, music recordings, or other creative works, allowing students to demonstrate their talents and achievements beyond academics.

Research Papers

For applicants to STEM-focused programs or those with a strong interest in undergraduate research, submitting a research paper or abstract can highlight their dedication to scholarly inquiry. Published works or those presented at conferences are ideal, but graded high school papers, such as the IB Extended Essay or the German 'Facharbeit,' can also be considered. These papers should communicate the hypothesis, methodology, findings, and conclusions, demonstrating the applicant's research abilities.

> Consider submitting your IB Extended Essay or German 'Facharbeit' as a research paper

Art and Performance Supplements

Artistic submissions are particularly relevant for art, music, dance, or theater majors. They can also be a valuable tool for applicants to liberal arts colleges, allowing them to highlight their artistic talents alongside academics. Art portfolios may include various mediums, such as paintings, drawings, sculpture, photography, and digital art, showcasing a range of techniques and artistic development. For performing arts programs, video recordings of musical performances, theater productions, or dance routines can capture the applicant's skill level, stage presence, and interpretative abilities.

> Artistic submissions are likely to be reviewed by faculty members, not admissions officers

Auditions for Fine Arts Programs

Auditions play a crucial role in admissions to obtain a Bachelor of Fine Arts, such as music, dance, theater, and sometimes film. Most colleges have specific requirements for prescreening materials, including the number of pieces, repertoire, and video quality. The recordings should have clear sound quality and adequate lighting, even if professional production is not necessary.

> Live auditions may be the most important factor in BFA admissions

Applicants who pass the prescreening are invited to perform a live audition to assess their technical skills, stage presence, and potential for growth. This is your chance to shine, so make sure you are thoroughly prepared. Rehearse your audition pieces and practice in mock auditions to simulate the experience and receive constructive feedback. Some programs offer virtual live auditions, which take place via video conferencing platforms. Before your virtual audition, ensure your internet connection is stable and your camera and microphone work well. Find a quiet, well-lit space where you can perform without interruptions and wear audition attire as if you were performing in person.

Other Creative Supplementals

Some colleges incorporate creative elements into their regular application process. For example, Rice University asks applicants to upload a photograph that captures an aspect of themselves not represented elsewhere in their application. While the 'Rice Box' is an opportunity to think outside the box (pun intended), it is best to choose an image that is relevant to your application. Do not waste this opportunity by uploading a silly picture – no photos of rice! – but try to find an original photo that reinforces your story. Other examples of creative supplemental materials requested by colleges include short stories, video essays, or a piece of original music.

The 'Rice Box' asks for one photograph without explanation

A few selective colleges encourage applicants to showcase their technical abilities through a maker portfolio. First introduced by MIT, this supplement allows students to demonstrate their technical creativity in the fields of engineering, computer science, and technology. This can include projects such as building a robot, designing a website, or creating a mobile app. Students may upload images, a video of up to 120 seconds, and one PDF of technical documentation via the app SlideRoom[105] to share a project completed outside of school.

Present your creative engineering projects in a maker portfolio

In general, it is crucial to verify the submission guidelines of each college, as they may use the Common App, their own portal, or external platforms like SlideRoom or Getacceptd[106]. Since admissions officers evaluate thousands of applications during one admissions cycle, be mindful before submitting optional supplementals – only provide material that adds value to your overall application.

International Specifics

The application process differs slightly for international students due to their diverse educational backgrounds and the requirement of obtaining a student visa. Most colleges define international students as those applicants who are not U.S. residents and need a visa to stay legally in the country. Still, it is advisable to verify the exact definition for each prospective institution to understand which student category applies to your specific situation.

Chapter 7 – Qualitative Components of an Application

-Translated transcripts
-Predicted grades for national exams
-English proficiency
-Financial resources
-F-1 student visa

Students whose native language is not English must demonstrate English proficiency unless they have studied for at least three years at a high school that primarily instructs in English. The TOEFL[107] and IELTS[108] exams are widely accepted as evidence of English proficiency; some colleges may also recognize Duolingo as an alternative. Students must self-report their scores in the 'Testing' section of the Common App and request in their TOEFL or IELTS accounts that official test scores be sent directly to all colleges they apply to. Remember to schedule and prepare for the examinations well in advance to ensure timely delivery of your scores before application deadlines.

Like domestic applicants, international students must submit both self-reported and official academic records from all high schools they attended. Students from countries following the United Kingdom education system must report their final exam scores, such as the General Certificate of Secondary Education or the A-levels, instead of internal school transcripts. If you need to pass final examinations to graduate from high school (A-levels, Abitur, Bac, etc.), you must enter your actual or predicted test scores and subjects in the section 'Senior Secondary Leaving Examinations' under the 'Testing' tab of the Common App. Certified translations must accompany all records that are not in English so admissions officers can understand the documents.

Students must enter final or predicted scores of national exams

To obtain an F-1 student visa, students must provide evidence that they can cover tuition and living costs during their first year of study. Before submitting their application, international students should check the website of the Department of Homeland Security[109] to ensure the prospective college is approved to sponsor F-1 student visas.

Chapter 8 – Admissions Considerations Beyond Academics

College admissions is a multifaceted process, where admissions officers must evaluate not only the quality of each application but also consider how each applicant fits into the bigger picture of a diverse incoming class. Beyond assessing academic performance, colleges must balance various other institutional needs. Financial considerations play a significant role, as universities must ensure a sustainable revenue stream. Athletic programs require a balanced roster across all teams, while the orchestra may need an additional harp player for their ensemble. Moreover, colleges seek to maintain strong alumni networks and foster a culture of philanthropy to support their operations.

> Understanding a college's priorities can help you tailor your application

The admissions process has many moving parts, and priorities may shift unpredictably from one year to the next. The specific dynamics of these considerations are unknown outside of the closed doors of university offices, making it difficult to account for them in the application process. However, college admissions is not a black box, at least not entirely. Most priorities and concerns are well-known within the higher education community, but the degree to which these factors are applied in the decision-making process is not transparent. Still, by understanding the critical considerations of admissions offices, you can better prepare your application and set realistic expectations for your chances of admission. While we may be unable to make the process completely transparent, understanding the various factors at play can help demystify the admissions process, turning the black box into a grey one instead. As knowledge is power, understanding key considerations will help you navigate the process, present yourself in the best possible light, and set realistic expectations for potential outcomes.

Institutional Priorities

A university's strategic goals and priorities guide the admissions office in selecting its future students. While academic excellence is the most apparent goal, colleges often have additional, more subtle priorities that guide the admissions process. Based on these priorities, colleges aim to build a well-rounded incoming class – a process known as 'shaping the class' – by assembling a variety of talents, experiences, and backgrounds to enrich the campus community. Institutions

> Institutional priorities are (mostly) unknown and may change from one year to the next

may prioritize applicants based on various factors such as diversity, athletic team quotas, or potential for future donations. Priorities vary from one institution to another and can even change from year to year based on evolving goals and needs.

Many colleges aim for a diverse student body that includes individuals from various racial, socio-economic, geographic, and cultural backgrounds, as well as different talents in arts, technology, and other

Chapter 8— Admissions Considerations Beyond Academics

areas. Admissions may also prioritize applicants based on their intended major, especially to balance enrollment across programs or to grow emerging fields within the institution. Some colleges also consider an applicant's likelihood to graduate by assessing their academic preparedness and the fit between the applicant's goals and what the college offers.

American colleges have a long tradition of emphasizing athletics. Sports teams bring in a lot of money through ticket sales and merchandise and improve a college's spirit and brand recognition. In addition, research links athletic performance with higher alumni donations. Some colleges consider an applicant's legacy status or potential financial contributions when rendering admissions decisions. Each institution faces a unique situation that influences the factors they consider in admissions.

Non-comprehensive list of institutional priorities:

→ First-generation students (first one to attend a college)
→ Underrepresented backgrounds (e.g., socio-economic status, race/ethnicity, LGBT+, gender, etc.)
→ Geographic diversity (e.g., certain rural states)
→ Applicants to under-enrolled academic programs or majors
→ Legacy applicants (family member attended the institution)
→ Children of faculty and staff
→ Athletes
→ Children of VIP (e.g., child of an influential politician or celebrity)
→ Potential or past donors
→ Special talents
→ Religious affiliation

Based on the four most common institutional priorities, colleges often categorize matching applicants as 'ALDC': athletes, legacy, dean's preferences, and children of faculty. In addition, most colleges also factor in lower-tier priorities in their decisions.

Institutional priorities can be compared to an iceberg. What colleges look for may seem transparent, but many admissions criteria remain hidden, like an iceberg's submerged bulk. The rigor of courses, GPA, standardized test scores, and extracurriculars are apparent factors. However, institutional priorities and the extent to which they shape admissions decisions remain mostly unclear and vary from one institution to another.

Iceberg of Institutional Priorities
Most admissions criteria are unknown and opaque

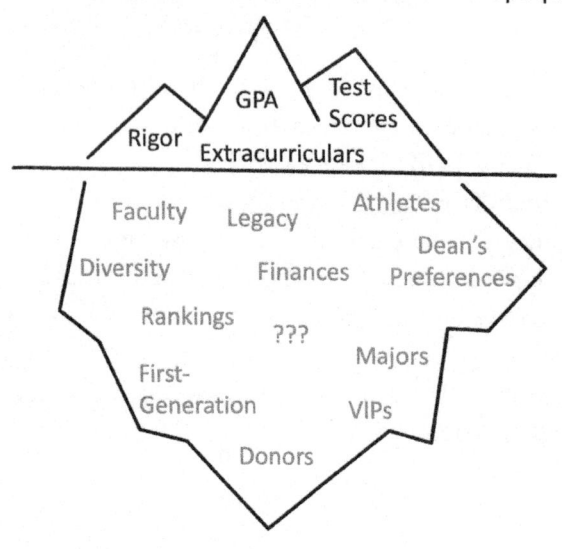

Above the waterline: Rigor, GPA, Test Scores, Extracurriculars

Below the waterline: Faculty, Legacy, Athletes, Diversity, Finances, Dean's Preferences, Rankings, ???, Majors, First-Generation, VIPs, Donors

Chapter 8— Admissions Considerations Beyond Academics

While institutional priorities may be opaque, you can unveil them through research. Exploring a college's website, mission statement, recent press releases, and their Common Data Set can provide valuable insights into their values and priorities. To access the CDS, enter 'college name' and 'common data set' into your Internet browser. Information sessions, campus tours, and conversations with admissions officers, alumni, or current students can provide additional clues about what a college values in its students.

> The CDS and college website give insights into institutional priorities

Once you are aware of a college's priorities, you can leverage this knowledge to tailor and strengthen your application. For example, you can highlight in your essays how your experiences and goals align with the college's priorities or how you can contribute to the campus community in meaningful ways. Understanding institutional priorities can guide you on how to present yourself in your application. At the same time, you may or may not fit into the institutional category that a college prioritizes in a given application cycle. Remember not to take rejections personally, as they are often influenced by institutional priorities and are not a reflection of your abilities or potential.

Diversity Considerations

Colleges view themselves as a microcosm of society and agents for upward social and economic mobility. By diversifying their student body, they provide underrepresented groups access to higher education, which can contribute to breaking the cycles of poverty and building a more equitable society.

Inspired by the Civil Rights Movement in the 1960s, many American colleges implemented a practice called 'affirmative action' to address historical injustices by providing opportunities for underrepresented groups. Under affirmative action, colleges considered race as one factor in their admissions process. However, in 2023, the United States Supreme Court delivered a landmark ruling that banned this practice. The ruling emphasized that the admissions process must be race-neutral, and institutions cannot grant preferential treatment to applicants based on race.

> Affirmative action promoted diversity by supporting historically underrepresented groups

The end of affirmative action forces colleges to reevaluate their admissions criteria and develop alternative strategies for achieving a diverse student body. After race-conscious admissions practices were banned in California in 1996, enrollment of underrepresented students at the University of California decreased, particularly at its most selective campuses, UC Berkeley and UCLA. In response, the UC system implemented various strategies to maintain diversity, such as holistic admissions policies, dedicated outreach programs, and guaranteed admission for the top-performing students in California. However, despite these extensive efforts, the UC campuses still do not reflect the racial diversity of California's high school population. This experience highlights the difficulties institutions face in achieving diversity without being able to directly consider an applicant's racial background during admissions.

> In 2023, the Supreme Court prohibited affirmative action

Chapter 8— Admissions Considerations Beyond Academics

Although California may provide a blueprint, we can only speculate how other institutions will modify their admissions practices to meet diversity goals without explicitly considering race or ethnicity. Options may include a greater emphasis on geographic location, personal adversity, or socioeconomic status as a proxy to achieve racial diversity indirectly. In addition, colleges may expand their outreach through mentorship or scholarship programs to encourage more applications from underrepresented groups.

> Essays, geographic location, adversity, or interviews may become means to achieve diversity

Qualitative elements in the application, like essays, interviews, or video submissions, may become more important. For instance, for its incoming class of 2025, Harvard University introduced a new mandatory supplemental question: *"Harvard has long recognized the importance of enrolling a diverse student body. How will the life experiences that shape who you are today enable you to contribute to Harvard?"*[110] Through this supplemental essay, Harvard's admissions officers aim to gauge how a candidate's unique background can help achieve their diversity objectives.

In the immediate future, as colleges adapt to the absence of affirmative action, new opportunities may arise for international students. Some colleges may consider admitting more international students to achieve a more diverse student body.

> Opportunities may arise for international applicants

Legacy Applicants

For decades, highly selective colleges have been providing a leg-up to children and relatives of alumni by favoring them in their admissions process. A legacy applicant typically has one or more immediate family members, such as a parent or sibling, who have graduated from the same institution. Secondary legacy sometimes extends to grandparents, aunts, uncles, and distant relatives. According to the Common Data Set, almost 800 colleges consider some legacy preference in their admissions process, resulting in significantly higher acceptance rates than non-legacy applicants.

> Legacy admit rates are two to ten times higher than for non-legacies

While the exact figures vary by institution, reports suggest that legacy applicants are admitted at two to ten times the rate of non-legacies. For example, Harvard's overall admit rate in 2022 was 3.2% compared to 34% for legacy applicants[111]. At the same time, children of donors and alumni were twenty times more likely to be interviewed by a Harvard admissions officer than non-legacy applicants. During a lawsuit accusing them of discrimination, Harvard had to disclose that they maintain a separate admissions process for children of legacy and other influential families. Applicants marked for the 'Dean's Interest List,' also known

Legacy perks:
- Higher admit rate
- One extra interview
- Pre-screening
- Mock interviews
- Special advising
- Dedicated officers
- Ear-marked scholarships
- Dean's interest list

Chapter 8— Admissions Considerations Beyond Academics

as the Z-list, are admitted based on the condition that they defer for one year.

Other examples of preferential treatment include the University of Southern California, where legacy applicants receive a 'special interest tag.' At Stanford University, legacy applicants undergo a dual review versus a single review for non-legacies, resulting in 16% of their incoming class of 2023 having legacy status[112]. Other perks for legacy applicants may include dedicated admissions officers, special advising sessions, mock or practice interviews, and dedicated scholarships for legacy applicants.

That being said, legacy admissions have come under fire for perpetuating inequality. Critics argue that this practice favors predominantly white and affluent applicants, thus undermining the principles of meritocracy. The recent Supreme Court ruling that struck down affirmative action has further fueled this debate. Shortly after the Supreme Court prohibited race-based admissions, civil rights groups filed a complaint against Harvard, alleging that its preferential treatment of legacy applicants systematically disadvantages applicants of color.

Several states have taken legislative steps in response to the growing discontent and various admissions scandals. For example, California enacted laws targeting 'admission by exception' policies, prohibiting public colleges from considering race and requiring private institutions to report on legacy admissions. Colorado banned legacy preferences in 2021, followed by Virginia and Maryland in spring 2024[113]. Individual institutions like the

Some colleges no longer consider legacy in admissions

University of Minnesota, Amherst College, and Pomona College have already eliminated legacy preferences, signaling a potential shift in the admissions landscape.

Recruited Athletes

Competitive sports are a fundamental aspect of American culture, and to that effect, American colleges celebrate their sports teams. It is common practice for colleges to recruit skilled athletes for their athletic departments, providing them with a dedicated path to admissions. This practice often surprises international families, and even in the U.S., the preferential treatment of athletes triggered a debate about the balance between athletic and academic merits.

> College sport is treasured for prestige, cultural, and monetary reasons

Promoting athletics is not only a tradition in the States, but there are many other reasons why colleges invest heavily in their athletic programs. Athletic events, especially in high-profile sports like football and basketball, can galvanize the entire campus and foster a strong school spirit. Athletic success can also enhance a college's national visibility through extensive media coverage, potentially boosting application numbers. In addition, sports programs can be financially lucrative through ticket sales, merchandise, broadcasting rights, and alumni donations. These financial gains fund not just the athletic department but also academic scholarships, campus improvements, and other educational initiatives, thereby benefiting the entire college community. Given the many advantages of college sports, many

Chapter 8— Admissions Considerations Beyond Academics

institutions have created dedicated admissions pathways for recruited athletes.

The Recruiting Process

The journey of a recruited athlete typically begins long before the college application season. To get noticed as a potential collegiate athlete, students must craft a comprehensive recruiting profile, showcasing their athletic and academic achievements to college coaches and recruiters. These profiles typically include personal information, contact details, academic qualifications, athletic statistics, sport-specific metrics, awards and recognitions, team memberships, video highlights, and a personal statement. Aspiring athletes can utilize platforms like Hudl[114] and the NCAA portal[115] to showcase their athletic talent through reels, statistics, and performance analysis.

> Maintain a strong recruiting profile to get noticed

Coaches begin scouting potential recruits as early as 9th grade, as they must plan for team or player succession well in advance. Recruiters look for positions that will need to be filled several years down the road when current athletes will graduate. They evaluate online recruiting profiles and attend games, meets, camps, or matches to assess the skills of potential candidates. Once a promising athlete is identified, the recruitment process may include personalized communication, campus visits, and formal offers to join the team, often accompanied by an athletic scholarship.

> Athletes may be recruited or have a hook in admissions

While recruited athletes may receive special consideration during the admissions process, they must still meet the minimum academic standards defined by the National Collegiate Athletic Association[116]. The admissions office and athletic department usually collaborate closely in evaluating recruited athletes. Coaches typically advocate for their recruits during the review process, providing assessments of their athletic abilities and potential contributions to the team. However, the final admissions decision rests with the admissions office, which considers the athlete's academic qualifications and athletic talent holistically.

Particularly at small-sized colleges with a significant emphasis on collegiate sports, a considerable portion of available incoming spots may be dedicated to athletes. For example, one-third of the 2,000 students attending Williams College in Massachusetts are athletes[117]. While not all athletes are actively recruited, team succession planning and the athletic ability of applicants are likely to be factors considered during admissions. Since sports teams have specific roster needs, colleges allocate a certain number of admissions slots to athletes, reducing the number of spots available for non-athlete applicants. Recruited athletes often commit to their colleges through early decision agreements or by signing a National Letter of Intent, which binds them to the institution and its athletic program. This commitment comes with the expectation that the athlete will contribute significantly to the team while balancing their sport with academic duties.

> Small colleges have a higher ratio of athletes to non-athletes than large universities

Chapter 8 — Admissions Considerations Beyond Academics

Organization in Divisions

Division 1: Large budgets including headcount scholarships

Division 2: Smaller, equivalency budgets

Division 3: Applicants are not recruited, but have a hook in admissions

The NCAA organizes college sports into three divisions, with Division 1 being the highest level. 363 colleges compete at the D1 level, emphasizing their athletic programs immensely. These schools allocate substantial budgets to attract top talent, enabling them to offer generous athletic scholarships. Highly sought-after athletes may be offered a 'full ride,' covering all expenses, including tuition and housing.

For D1 student-athletes, their sport becomes a near full-time commitment, with extensive practice schedules often leaving little time for other pursuits. Some colleges may even restrict the academic majors available to their athletes. D1 coaches have a significant influence on the admissions process, securing dedicated slots for their recruited athletes. As of spring 2024, significant changes could be on the horizon for collegiate sports. A landmark settlement[118] involving the NCAA is expected to revolutionize the compensation structure,

Headcount or full-ride scholarships for D1 football, basketball, volleyball, gymnastics, and tennis allowing D1 athletes to earn money for their performance instead of playing just for scholarships and exposure.

The 313 Division 2 colleges demand a less intensive time commitment from their athletes. Operating with smaller budgets, they distribute scholarships more evenly across all athletes, typically in the form of partial or equivalency scholarships; this means that full rides are not likely. Division 3, the largest division with 442 participating colleges, aims to balance athletics and academics. While D3 schools do not offer athletic scholarships, high-performing student-athletes can receive preferential consideration during admissions due to the value they bring to the athletic program.

> Equivalency = scholarships that split the budget across multiple athletes

More recently, esports, or competitive video gaming, has grown significantly, with approximately 250 colleges offering varsity esports programs[119]. These programs are structured similarly to traditional sports programs, with teams, coaches, and competitions. Top esports games include Call of Duty, Counter-Strike, Dota 2, Fortnite, League of Legends, and Valorant.

Financial Considerations

From a bird's-eye perspective, the American landscape of higher education is increasingly divided. On one side, we have financially stable colleges, with massive endowments in the billions. With robust financials, these institutions are shielded from fiscal pressures and can attract top talent by providing generous financial aid packages.

Chapter 8— Admissions Considerations Beyond Academics

Unsurprisingly, they are inundated with applications, further enhancing their appeal.

On the other hand, some lower-tier colleges face challenges due to a lack of financial stability. Escalating operating costs and declining enrollment numbers pose a real threat, potentially compromising the quality of education they can provide. The situation creates a self-perpetuating cycle. As financial stability becomes a crucial factor in students' college decisions, applicants are drawn to institutions perceived as financially secure. Colleges with declining enrollment face financial challenges, which may further deter potential applicants, creating a vicious cycle. As enrollment numbers diminish, colleges may struggle to generate sufficient revenue, leading to budget constraints that impact academic programs, campus facilities, and student services. These limitations make the institution less appealing to prospective students, exacerbating the enrollment decline. To counter this downward spiral, these colleges may admit more applicants who do not require financial aid and can pay the full tuition rate.

> Colleges must manage their revenues and expenses to maintain financial stability

In addition, admissions policies can influence decisions. Unless a college is need-blind and does not examine a student's ability to pay the full tuition, finances are one factor that admissions officers consider. Colleges must balance their need for financial stability with their mission to provide access to education. Consequently,

> Many colleges consider a student's ability to pay full price

admission officers typically assess the financial status of applicants during the admissions process. This does not mean that only affluent students are admitted, but colleges seek a balanced mix of students who can pay the sticker price and those who need financial aid.

Colleges with large endowments can afford generous financial assistance

Colleges use financial aid packages to make education accessible to students from different economic backgrounds and to attract top talent; both aspects can affect the institution's rankings and reputation. However, the amount of financial aid a college can offer is typically tied to its financial policies, public funding, and endowments.

Particularly, the size of a college's endowment can significantly impact its ability to attract talent and offer merit-based aid. On the other hand, public institutions are subject to the influence of state and federal funding, which can fluctuate based on political and economic factors. Changes in funding can directly affect tuition rates, financial aid packages, and even the number of students an institution can enroll.

Top Five Endowments in 2021 [120]

Harvard:	$ 53 billion
Yale:	$ 43 billion
U of Texas:	$ 40 billion
Stanford:	$ 38 billion
Princeton:	$ 37 billion

Chapter 8— Admissions Considerations Beyond Academics

Yield management, the strategy used to ensure 100% enrollment, is another factor in a college's financial considerations. Colleges aim to accept students likely to enroll because a higher yield rate can improve the school's ranking and desirability. To protect their yield, institutions may deny highly qualified applicants who they suspect will not attend. Without the correct algorithm to protect their yield while ensuring 100% enrollment, colleges jeopardize their financial viability, as they may be unable to fill all spots of their incoming class. Vacant spots directly undermine their financials due to the loss of tuition revenue. Being rejected by a safety school may feel incomprehensible for a qualified applicant but the decision may be driven by the college's efforts to maximize its yield and protect its financials.

A college's financial viability, endowment size, and yield management can impact admissions decisions. However, amidst the financial strains experienced by some colleges, there could be positive implications for international and out-of-state students.

> Higher tuition rates make out-of-state and international students attractive to public colleges

These applicants, who usually pay higher tuition rates, may be seen as attractive candidates and could serve as a considerable source of revenue, potentially increasing their chances of admission.

Evaluating Applicants Within Their Local Context

Every individual is unique, and not all students have access to the same opportunities, making it challenging to assess a pool of applicants in a fair and consistent manner. Whether a student attends a well-endowed private school with a long list of available AP courses or a small, rural, and underfunded public high school, their individual circumstances are taken into account. Admissions officers evaluate each student within their local context. But how do colleges gain insight into individual opportunities and external constraints?

> Colleges assess applicants within their local context

Colleges assess applicants within their local context, which refers to the unique circumstances and opportunities available to students in their specific geographic region or high school. This approach ensures that each applicant is evaluated fairly, considering the resources and challenges they may have faced.

Applicants with similar backgrounds are evaluated collectively as a group. These groups may encompass students from the same high school, geographical region, or, in the case of international students, an entire country. During these reviews, admissions officers try to understand how students from the same environment have used the opportunities available to them. To what extent did a student challenge themselves academically by taking advanced classes? Have they found other ways to dive deeper into a subject, such as online courses, summer classes,

> How well did a student use the resources available to them?

or taking courses at a community college? Did they participate in, lead, or launch a club or school activity? How does an applicant compare to others from the same background? Basically, the admissions office evaluates how much the applicant utilized the available resources to

Chapter 8— Admissions Considerations Beyond Academics

expand their skills and experiences in comparison to other students sharing the same context.

Most admissions teams are structured in a way that allows them to familiarize themselves with the diverse backgrounds of their applicants. Each admissions officer usually specializes in a specific geographic region. As they review thousands of applications from the same area, admissions officers naturally become familiar with local contexts. Through research, perusing school profiles, participating in college fairs, and conducting school visits, the officer understands the opportunities a high school offers its students. This expertise in the local context ensures that colleges do not penalize students

> Specialized admissions officers are familiar with the opportunities available to students

for having fewer opportunities available to them. By understanding their local context, admission officers can better evaluate how well an applicant has used available resources and opportunities. This brings us to the next chapter, which examines possible strategies for enhancing your profile and increases your chances of being admitted.

Chapter 9 – Improving Your Profile

Here is the million-dollar question: How can you improve your application profile to increase your chances of acceptance? College preparatory and admissions consulting businesses flourish worldwide and have become a multibillion-dollar industry. College consultants and independent educational counselors offer a full suite of services to guide families through the college application process. While some elite consultants charge hundreds of dollars per hour, others provide complete packages for $5-10,000 and more. These intensive services are clearly beyond the scope of this handbook. Nevertheless, understanding the admissions process and possible decision criteria will help you make smart choices and improve your profile. Let us start by looking at how admissions offices evaluate their applicants.

> Knowledge is power and helps you boost your profile

Academic Rigor: Depth and Breadth

As educational institutions, colleges primarily aim to promote knowledge and academic advancement. Therefore, one of the key criteria admissions officers seek in high school students is academic rigor. In college admissions, rigor refers to the level of academic challenge – the depth and breadth in a student's high school courses. A rigorous academic profile involves demanding coursework, such as honors, AP,

Chapter 9— Improving Your Profile

or dual enrollment classes, demonstrating that students challenge themselves in their academic work. Applicants with a consistent record of academic rigor are more likely to thrive in their college education and emerge as successful alumni.

While standardized tests like the SAT provide insights into how a student fares academically compared to other applicants, they are only a short snapshot of performance. With the recent trend of test-optional policies, colleges began to place greater emphasis on a student's high school transcript and GPA. Admissions officers understand the applicant's local context through the school profile and counselor letter. The course load indicates how much a student has stretched themselves academically, while the GPA indicates how successful they were in the selected courses.

Maximizing your academic rigor helps improve your profile, as it demonstrates your academic aptitude and curiosity. At the same time, you must maintain good grades, as a lower GPA may prevent you from moving on to the next step in the admissions process. Getting an 'A' in a less rigorous course may be more advantageous than a 'C' in an AP class. The rule of thumb is to take the highest number of advanced courses that you can handle while maintaining a good GPA. Let us look at how this general guideline translates into specific choices you make during your high school years.

> Maximize your academic rigor while protecting your GPA

Academic Depth

Let us first examine academic depth, the level of expertise you gain in a particular subject through advanced classes. By diving deep into a topic, you gain a profound understanding of the field, its concepts, and methodologies. Demonstrating academic depth signals to a college that you are willing to challenge yourself academically and will likely thrive in their academic environment.

One way to showcase academic depth is by taking advanced classes. If offered, take honors, AP, or IB courses instead of the regular ones, assuming you can handle their complexity. Some students decide to skip the College Board's AP exam in May. However, taking the exam has no downside. Passing an AP exam with a score of 3 or higher indicates that you are ready to handle college-level work and can retain the content of a challenging, year-long course. In addition, you can choose whether to report the scores later in your college application.

Dive deep into one subject

Some experts recommend checking a college's website to find which AP scores they accept for credit and report only these or higher scores. However, if you do not sit for the AP exam or do not report the results, the admissions officer will likely assume a failing score. By not submitting an AP score, the admissions officer may think you did worse in the exam than you actually did. If your AP exam score does not represent your performance in the AP course on your transcript, you can provide some background in one of your essays. Alternatively, you may ask your subject teacher to

Do not just take the class; sit for the AP exam

Chapter 9— Improving Your Profile

attest to your academic performance in the course through a letter of recommendation. In general, it raises a red flag if you do not explain any discrepancies in your profile, and admissions officers may draw the wrong conclusion when you do not offer an explanation yourself.

Another way to enhance your academic depth is to explore opportunities outside school. For example, you can self-study for an AP exam if your high school does not offer it. Self-studying allows you to learn at your own pace and dive deeper into subjects

> Use opportunities outside of your high school

that interest you. However, you must have a high degree of self-discipline to complete the coursework independently. If you prefer more support, consider attending an online AP course at an accredited company. These classes provide structured learning environments and access to experienced instructors. For example, UC Scout[121] provides multiple classes approved by the University of California, and Khan Academy[122] offers free test preparation and AP courses. This proactive approach demonstrates your initiative and genuine interest in expanding your knowledge.

> AP > IB > honors > regular classes

While there is no general formula for how colleges assess an applicant's academic depth, there are some considerations. AP and IB classes are considered the most rigorous since they use a standardized curriculum and end in a centralized exam. However, the College Board offers more AP classes than the IB curriculum, allowing students to enroll in more advanced courses through the AP program than IB. Therefore, AP classes are usually considered the most impactful courses. Remember, the goal is to do your best in the highest classes you can take without sacrificing your GPA, so choose your classes wisely and focus on your academic strengths.

Academic Breadth

The second dimension demonstrating rigor is academic breadth, the number of classes taken from various fields. While focusing extensively on one specific area exhibits your academic depth, you can showcase academic breadth by taking courses beyond your main area of interest. Colleges seek well-rounded students who expand their knowledge beyond their obvious strengths. Use electives to expand your breadth, including areas that may be atypical for your major, such as adding some music classes if you plan to apply as a math major.

> Study a wide range of subjects

Consider taking additional courses at local community colleges. Even if not all colleges accept these courses for credit, it shows that you challenge yourself and expand your horizons beyond what is available at your high school. Typically, colleges look for four years of the core subjects: English, math, sciences, social studies, and a foreign language. Some colleges, such as CalPoly in San Luis Obispo, even recommend at least five years of high school math and English courses. This can be accomplished by either taking Algebra 1 in middle school or through dual enrollment at a community college.

> Most colleges expect four years of classes in the core subjects

Even if you have already fulfilled most of the graduation requirements as a high school junior, take a full load of academic courses in your senior year, including advanced classes. 'Senioritis,' the motivational decline during 12th grade, is a real phenomenon, but it is important to finish strong. It is rare but not unheard of that colleges, especially highly selective ones, rescind their offers when a student's performance in senior year spirals out of control. If anything, colleges prefer to see upward trajectories for grades and GPA.

Reasons Not to Reject You

Do you remember the massive increase in applications in the past 20 years? With thousands of applications to review, admissions officers spend an average of eight minutes reading an application[123]. Since you only have a few minutes to impress them, it is essential to have a concise and coherent story demonstrating that you...

GPA, academic rigor, and standardized tests are the gatekeepers

    a) ... can handle the academics,
    b) ... will add value to their campus life, and
    c) ... will become a successful and engaged alumni.

During the holistic review process, your academic rigor and aptitude, as demonstrated by your course selection, grades, GPA, and standardized test scores, are the initial gatekeepers. Meeting a college's minimum academic standard is not just important, it is critical to avoid immediate rejection. Colleges aim to admit students who can handle their academics and thrive at their institution and beyond.

At the same time, colleges are cautious not to compromise their academic standards and rankings by admitting too many students with lower academic scores. The Common Data Set[124] contains a plethora of college-specific statistics, allowing students to estimate the academic expectations of a particular college. The CDS provides detailed information about admission statistics, student demographics, and financial aid options. It also reveals how much weight a college attributes to different application elements, such as grades, essays, or letters of recommendation. Analyzing the CDS data can shed some light on what accounts for safety, target, and reach schools and helps estimate one's admission chances.

> Academic performance is the reason not to reject you – but it may not be enough to get admitted

> The CDS helps you understand what a college is looking for

While applicants must include their GPA, courses, and grades in their application, many colleges still have test-optional policies, leaving it up to the applicant whether they submit their standardized test scores. However, if included in the application, the admissions officers will consider them in their admissions decisions. This flexibility begs the – difficult – question of whether to submit or withhold one's scores.

To Submit or Not to Submit?

First, let us address the elephant in the room. To even consider this question, you must have taken a standardized exam, ideally multiple

Chapter 9— Improving Your Profile

times. Unless you plan to exclusively apply to test-blind schools, you should sit for standardized exams. Just do it. Use free practice exams to decide which test, the SAT or ACT, suits you best. Always prepare before sitting for an exam, as it is key to achieving your best scores. While some colleges let you combine the highest scores of each section for a so-called 'super score,' others may require you to send the scores of all exams you have taken. Going into the exam unprepared could lower your overall scores for those colleges requesting all test results.

After achieving your highest score, you must determine whether submitting it to a test-optional college will enhance or detract from your application. To do this, examine the ranges of previously admitted students in the college's Common Data Set. This statistic provides insight into how many students were admitted with a specific range for GPA and test scores, helping you gauge your chances of admission. The general agreement is to submit test scores if they fall within a college's competitive range. To be competitive, your scores should rank in the upper quartile of the range, indicating that you are among the top 25% of previously admitted students. At the very least, they should exceed the mean of past scores. However, refrain from submitting your scores if they fall below the 50th percentile, as they are likely to impact your application negatively.

> Submit your SAT/ACT scores if they are in the top 25% to 50% of previously admitted students

While the test-optional policies were supposed to alleviate the challenges of the pandemic, they added another layer of complexity to the admissions process. The decision of whether to submit one's scores has become a strategic question in the maze of college admissions.

Studies show that students in underperforming high schools particularly withhold their scores when they are below a college's threshold. However, as students are judged within the local context of their school, withholding their scores may occasionally work against them. For instance, a student with an SAT score of 1300 may choose not to submit it to a highly competitive college where the mean is 1450. If the average SAT score at the student's high school is 1000, indicating that they outperformed their peers by 300 points, the student's score of 1300 may actually enhance their profile, even if it is below the college average of 1450. In such cases, not submitting a solid but not stellar score may potentially work against you. When deciding whether to submit test scores, you should consider both the average scores of previously admitted students as well as your own performance in the local context.

> Standardized performance is assessed in the local context

Recent trends in the admissions landscape suggest a reevaluation of test-optional policies. MIT, Georgetown, and the University of Florida had already returned to mandating test scores to apply. In February 2024, Dartmouth College announced the reinstatement of its mandatory testing policy[125], citing research indicating the value of standardized tests in identifying high-performing students, especially for applicants from low-income or lesser-known high schools. Beginning in fall 2024, U.S. applicants to Dartmouth must provide SAT or ACT scores, while international students require SAT, ACT, three AP exams, or their predicted IB, A-

> The pendulum seems to swing back toward requiring test scores

level, or other national exam scores to apply. Only a few days later, Yale[126] announced their new test-flexible policy, which requires applicants to submit either SAT, ACT, AP, or IB test results, and Brown followed suit in March 2024. With the first Ivy League colleges returning to standardized testing, the pendulum may swing back from test-optional policies to mandatory testing in the near future.

Reasons to Admit You

We already discussed the gatekeepers – GPA, academic rigor, and standardized tests – and their significance in preventing your application from being immediately rejected. Suppose your application has progressed to the next stage, the holistic review. Now, let us examine how you can best present the reasons why a college should admit you. While you cannot change a college's institutional priorities or influence the quality of applications of other applicants, several strategies exist to enhance your profile and craft a compelling application.

Passion Projects

In the competitive landscape of college admissions, one way to distinguish yourself is by presenting a unique talent or engagement that 'hooks' the admissions officer to your profile. A passion project – a personal endeavor driven by genuine enthusiasm – can achieve this by demonstrating your leadership skills, creativity, and dedication to pursuing your interests beyond the

A passion project may provide a hook for admissions

classroom. Colleges value these projects as they provide insights into applicants' values and potential contributions to the campus community.

Unlike school assignments, the student initiates, develops, and executes a passion project. As the name suggests, it focuses on an area the student feels deeply passionate about. These projects can range from starting a nonprofit organization, creating a mobile app, or conducting independent research to launching a small business or an art exhibition. Ideally, the project should have tangible outcomes, whether on the student's personal growth, their community, or even on a larger scale. Successfully executing such a project on top of other responsibilities like school or family chores requires resilience, problem-solving, and leadership skills – all attractive qualities to admissions committees.

Time is a critical factor in creating an impactful passion project. The more time invested, the more opportunities there are to learn, create something meaningful, and showcase genuine engagement. Begin well before your junior year to ensure ample time for meaningful development and to avoid conflicts with schoolwork and college applications. An early start also helps prevent admissions officers from perceiving your project as solely application-driven rather than genuine interest. With more time, you can research extensively and refine your approach to achieve a more polished and effective outcome. Recording your progress, challenges, and achievements will be invaluable when describing the project in essays. Executing a meaningful passion project allows you to provide a narrative to your application, provides a tangible example of

> Start early, as time is your biggest asset

how you can contribute to a college's community, and may provide you with a hook in the admissions process.

Demonstrated Interest

Showing your excitement for a particular college is another way to boost your application. Demonstrated interest, which is colloquially recognized as 'Tufts syndrome,' is another strategy to help you stand out. Tufts University, a popular safety school for Ivy League applicants, was one of the first colleges to include this practice in their admissions process. When analyzing their past data, Tufts noticed that admitted applicants with minimal engagement during the application process were unlikely to enroll. Concerned with protecting its

> Colleges track demonstrated interest to identify applicants likely to enroll

yield, admissions officers began tracking applicants' interest to gauge their likelihood of committing. Consequently, a lack of demonstrating interest may result in highly qualified applicants being 'yield protected,' meaning that the college rejects them, as they believe the students are likely to attend a more prestigious institution.

> Check the CDS ('level of applicant's interest' in section C7)

While some colleges prioritize demonstrated interest and meticulously track it, others do not consider it. Highly selective, prestigious colleges do not need to verify motivation – they just assume that admitted students will be over the moon and more than happy to enroll. However, smaller or less known colleges, particularly those considered a 'safety school' for top applicants, may track demonstrated interest to identify those truly enthusiastic about joining their institution. While it may not be the sole deciding factor, demonstrated interest can sway the decision when admissions officers are on the fence about an applicant. Therefore, consult the Common Data Set to verify how much a college values demonstrated interest and plan your engagement efforts accordingly.

There are numerous ways to demonstrate your interest in a particular college. Visiting a college campus in person is a strong indicator of interest. College tours, information sessions, and meetings with admissions representatives can show that you are serious about attending the college. Sign up for a virtual event if you cannot travel for an in-person campus tour. Applying through an early admissions program signals that the college is your top choice; since it is legally binding, applying through ED is the ultimate sign of demonstrated interest. Meaningful communication with the admissions office, whether through emails asking insightful questions or responding promptly to any correspondence from the college, can also show your genuine interest.

Don't apply in stealth mode!

Instead of using the general admissions email account, find out who the admissions representative for your area is and communicate directly with them. You do not want to apply in stealth mode, where your first interaction with a college is through the Common App. Speaking with college representatives at high school visits or college fairs can also show your interest in a college. Do not forget to scan your barcode so the college representative has a track record of speaking with you. Follow a college's social media accounts, and promptly open any emails you receive. When the email contains a link to the college website, click on it and explore the information. Usually, colleges track the number of times you visit their website or the duration of your visits. You will learn more about the college, and your interest will be tracked through the college's online statistics and saved in your admissions file.

Extracurricular Activities

Admissions officers view activities outside of high school academics as extracurriculars, which can impact admissions decisions by showcasing qualities not apparent from transcripts alone. For example, students with outstanding academic achievements but little or no community involvement may raise questions about their social engagement beyond personal success. Conversely, a student with average academics can enhance their application with a strong record of community service.

Impactful extracurriculars demonstrate personal development, leadership skills, and the ability to manage multiple commitments effectively alongside schoolwork. Commitment and leadership in a few select activities often outweigh the appearance of being a jack-of-all-trades; admissions offices seek evidence of long-term, focused commitment rather than fragmented engagements. Highlighting progression to leadership roles, such as advancing to club officer or team captain, provides tangible proof of your ability to lead and inspire others. Founding a club or leading significant projects demonstrates initiative and a willingness to take on

> Show commitment, progression, and leadership in your activities

challenges. Like so often in life, quality outweighs quantity. The significance of your involvement matters more than filling every field in the Common App. Do not just engage in something because you think it will look good in your college applications; with years of experience, most admissions officers can spot such an opportunistic approach. Included planned activities during 12th grade but avoid exaggerated entries.

Examples of extracurricular activities:

- → Unpaid internships
- → Paid part-time jobs
- → Non-academic clubs
- → Family responsibilities
- → Sports, music, theater, arts
- → Tutoring
- → Video gaming and esports
- → Volunteering
- → Competitions and contests

Some colleges segment extracurricular activities into multiple tiers. The top tier includes activities with achievements at the national or international level, while the most common activities, like club memberships, routine volunteer work, or participation in sports or arts without significant recognition, fall in the lowest tier. Still, even these activities can add value to your application by presenting you as a

> Go deep into activities that bolster your profile

well-rounded individual with diverse interests. For instance, managing a film blog can highlight your creativity, and volunteering at a local food bank demonstrates your social responsibility. Your activity list is also a great starting point to identify topics for your essays, and if you feel that you lack involvement in extracurriculars, you may address this in an essay response. With that being said, let us look closer at two particularly impactful extracurriculars that can help you stand out –volunteering and contests and competitions.

Contests and Competitions

While both involve a certain level of rivalry, the main difference between contests and competitions lies in their assessment structures. A contest emphasizes individual skill and is judged subjectively. Examples of contests include talent shows, art competitions, and essay contests. On the other hand, a competition involves a direct performance comparison with a clear winner based on objective criteria, such as sports events and academic competitions like spelling bees or math Olympiads.

Well-known competitions and contests:
- → Academic Decathlon
- → Chemistry / Math/ Science Olympiads
- → First Robotics Competition
- → Future Business Leaders of America
- → Harvard / MIT Math Tournament
- → International Science & Engineering Fair
- → Microsoft Imagine Cup
- → Model United Nations

- → National Economics Challenge
- → National French / German / Latin / Spanish exams
- → National Mock Trial
- → Regeneron International Science & Engineering Fair

Admissions officers value achievements in contests and competitions as they provide a fuller picture of an applicant's potential to contribute meaningfully to the campus community. Success in a competition demonstrates commitment and resilience and provides a benchmark for a student's performance relative to their peers. This is especially useful in assessing international applicants from different educational backgrounds or grading systems.

The experiences you gained from participating in a contest or competition are not just valuable in themselves, but they also make great topics for college essays. Reflect on the lessons learned, and use your experiences as evidence for your motivations, accomplishments, or any challenges you have overcome. By incorporating your involvement in a competition or contest into your essay, you make it more compelling, adhering to the guiding principle of 'show, don't tell.' You can demonstrate your drive and suitability by giving specific examples instead of making general declarations ('telling'). For the biggest impact, focus on competitions that align most closely with your interests and intended major.

> Reflect on your experiences at competitions in your essays

Chapter 9— Improving Your Profile

Volunteering

Colleges seek movers and shakers – individuals who recognize their capacity for meaningful change and take the initiative to make it happen. Volunteering can help you stand out by illustrating awareness of broader societal issues and proactive efforts to address them. Volunteer work indicates compassion and a likelihood to contribute to the campus environment. Volunteering often presents leadership opportunities through organizing events, leading projects, or even starting new initiatives. Earning recognition like the *Presidential Volunteer Service Award*[127], which the U.S. President awards to individuals volunteering between 50 and 250 hours in one year, can significantly enhance your application. As an international applicant, you can identify local volunteer opportunities.

Aim for 50 + volunteer hours

Although volunteering in diverse environments can broaden one's perspectives, local community engagement often holds more value than international service trips. Admissions officers are increasingly aware of the issues associated with 'pay to play' programs, as they tend to benefit affluent students who can afford the costs of organized international service trips. Making a positive impact can be done without traveling to another country. Your ongoing local engagement, where you can directly address regional concerns, may be viewed more favorably than expensive, short-term excursions abroad.

Potential volunteering opportunities:

- → American Red Cross
- → Animal shelters
- → Big Brothers Big Sisters of America
- → Environmental organizations
- → Food banks and soup kitchens
- → Hospitals and nursing homes
- → International organizations
- → Libraries and museums
- → Political campaigns
- → Religious institutions
- → Schools and summer camps

Choose volunteer activities that reflect your genuine interest and values. An authentic, long-term dedication to one cause is more impactful than superficial, random, or short engagements – for your personal development and in the eyes of admissions committees. Align your volunteer efforts with your academic and career aspirations. For example, volunteering at a veterinary clinic or animal shelter can give an aspiring veterinarian a reality check of the demands of the future job. The depth of your engagement, measured in total hours and the number of years, and the authenticity of your engagement are more meaningful than random, short-term volunteering gigs.

> List volunteer hours as community service in the Common App's activity section

Chapter 10 – Tips for Writing Your Essays

Admissions officers read thousands of essays each admissions cycle, making it all the more important that yours stand out. Your essays offer a glimpse into your personality, values, and how you engage with the world. Your choice of topics, the anecdotes you share, and your level of self-reflection contribute to making your essay distinctly yours. Remember, the essay should share a part of yourself that is not visible through your grades or test scores. Whether it is a story about a small moment that had a big impact on you, a passion that drives you, or a challenge you have overcome, presenting it through an authentic voice will make your essay resonate with the admissions committee.

> Your essays transform you into a real person

General Writing Strategies

Employing effective writing strategies can help you write your best essays. A compelling college essay tells a story – your story. Give yourself plenty of time to think about what you want to convey. Brainstorm ideas that represent your unique experiences, personality, and aspirations. Colleges are interested in what you have learned from your experiences, so include a reflection that showcases self-awareness and personal growth.

Writing in your authentic voice and staying true to yourself is paramount. Do not write what you believe admissions officers want to read but choose a topic that allows you to share something profound about yourself. How you articulate your message is just as important as the topic itself.

> Expect your essays to be checked for plagiarism and AI

While you may have many achievements and experiences, a concise essay diving into a single topic can be more revealing than skimming the surface of many. Whether you choose a narrative structure to tell a story or a thematic approach to highlight different facets of your experience, remember to illustrate your points with specific examples. These details will bring your story to life, making your response more memorable. A well-organized essay with a clear introduction, body, and conclusion helps convey your message effectively.

> Start early and revise your essay

Your English teacher was right: good writing involves revision. Review and edit your essay multiple times and consider feedback from parents, trusted teachers, or friends. Their perspectives can help you identify areas for improvement and ensure your essay is clear and compelling. Ensure readability by paying attention to proper grammar and punctuation. Proofread your essay carefully, and then, proofread it again. Reading your essay aloud is also a great way to identify any coherence, flow, or grammar issues. This approach allows you to produce a more thoughtful and polished essay.

Ensure you cover all aspects of the prompt directly and resist the temptation to reuse an essay for multiple applications. Tailor your response to each college, demonstrating knowledge of and interest in their unique programs, values, and community. For colleges requiring multiple essays, make sure that each one emphasizes a unique aspect of you; every response presents an opportunity for the admissions team to discover something fresh about you.

Address all parts of the prompt

Topics to Avoid

Crafting your essay is not just about choosing the right topic; knowing which subjects to avoid is equally important. Steer clear of clichés and extremely common narratives – admissions officers have seen them countless times. Unless you can provide a fresh perspective or demonstrate significant personal growth, these subjects are unlikely to let you stand out. Declaring your intentions to solve world hunger can seem naïve; discussing how a mission trip opened your eyes to social justice may come across as a perspective of privilege. Generally, avoid topics with a ubiquitous theme like 'the sports injury,' 'the mission trip,' 'lessons from the less fortunate,' or 'my immigrant family.' Phrases like 'I learned the true meaning of hard work,' or stories about 'the big game' can feel worn out. Instead, focus on presenting your experiences in a way that highlights your unique perspective and the personal growth you have achieved.

Avoid clichés and overused topics

While being authentic in your essay is critical, it is equally important to avoid overly personal issues such as intimate relationships and inappropriate topics like illegal activities. Sharing a personal challenge can demonstrate your resilience but is counterproductive when you focus solely on negative aspects or blame others for your shortcomings. It is crucial to frame difficulties in the context of growth and how they have led to positive outcomes or lessons learned.

Mental health is an important issue, but the college essay may not be the best platform. Despite increasing awareness, misunderstandings and stigma persist, which may influence the reader's perception of your readiness for the college environment. If you choose to address these sensitive topics, do so with care and consider how they fit into the broader narrative of your application. For instance, instead of focusing on your personal struggles with mental health, you could discuss your involvement in a mental health advocacy group and how it has shaped your perspective. Essays that touch on controversial subjects like politics and religion can also be risky, as they may alienate readers with different views. If you write about a controversial issue, strive for a balanced discussion demonstrating critical thinking and respect for diverse perspectives.

Stay clear of controversial topics

Exercise caution when using humor

Using humor to underline your personality or lighten the mood is another risky strategy. What is funny to you may not be to someone else. If you choose to include humor, ensure it is appropriate and does not detract from your overall message. In addition to these generic writing strategies, let us examine how to approach the three most important types of college essays: the personal statement, the personal insight questions, and the 'Why Us?' essay.

The Personal Statement

> Grades represent your past.
> The personal statement looks into your future.

The personal statement, a cornerstone of your application, is your space to share who you are in up to 650 words. It is not just an essay; it is your opportunity to present your story, showcase your personal growth, and outline what you will bring to the college community. Unlike other application components that reflect your past achievements, the personal statement is a platform to highlight your current identity and future potential. College admissions officers aim to discover three critical aspects through your essay: your unique personality, writing skills, and potential to enrich the campus community.

Structure your essay in a montage or chronologically

When organizing your personal statement, you can choose between two different approaches. A narrative structure tells a story where you start from the beginning and move toward the end. On the other hand, a montage is like creating a collage, where you pick different aspects of your life and connect them based on a common theme. This choice offers creative ways of weaving various aspects of your life together. Regardless of the structure, ensure each paragraph transitions smoothly to the next, and every section builds upon the last to create a cohesive narrative.

Crafting an engaging opening hook for your personal statement is crucial in capturing the attention of admissions officers. The opening paragraph sets the tone for the rest of the essay, establishes a personal connection with the reader, and motivates them to continue reading.

Possible options for a compelling opening:

- → a transformative experience that shaped your worldview, values, or goals
- → a specific anecdote that encapsulates your character, interests, or aspirations
- → a thought-provoking question that challenges the reader's expectations and sparks curiosity
- → a vivid scene that places the reader amid an important moment in your life
- → a quote that has influenced your life or thinking
- → an intriguing fact or an unusual achievement that offers insight into your character, interests, or ambitions
- → a quirky fact about yourself that can be a gateway into discussing the values, hobbies, or experiences that define you

Use the hook from your introduction as a springboard to dive deeper into your narrative. If you start with an anecdote, reflection, or a moment of realization, you flesh out these experiences in the essay's body. Provide more context, use specific examples, and explain why this

Chapter 10— Tips for Writing Your Essays

experience is significant. Organize the essay's body in a clear and logical manner.

The guiding principle for writing the personal statement is 'show, don't tell.' Through this writing technique, you demonstrate your qualities, experiences, and motivations through vivid and specific examples rather than simply stating them outright. When you 'show' rather than 'tell,' you paint a picture for the reader through descriptive storytelling. For example, instead of saying, 'I am hardworking and determined,' you may recount a specific instance where you demonstrated these qualities, such as persevering through a challenging project. By incorporating detailed anecdotes and examples, you bring your experiences to life, letting the reader experience your journey firsthand. This approach makes your essay more engaging and provides concrete evidence to support your claims.

> Show, don't tell!

Reflection is another critical component of the personal statement – it is not enough to just recount your experiences. This allows the admissions committee to see the depth of your character and how you have grown from your experiences. Connect your past experiences with your ambitions for the future. Focus on the impact each experience has had on you and how it has prepared you for the challenges and opportunities you may face in college. When crafting your essay, employing the "so what?" question is an effective technique to verify that your writing is reflective. This question prompts you to think about the significance of

> Connect your past experiences with your ambitions for the future

your experiences and how they have shaped you, adding depth and meaning to your essay.

Remember, the goal is to provide a deeper insight into who you are, how you think, and what you value. Be genuine and use concise language without jargon or overly complex sentences. Your personal statement is not about impressing the admissions committee with big words or grandiose stories but about sharing your true self. Take your time to revise and include feedback from a few trusted people. By articulating your experiences and reflections effectively in the personal statement, you can create a compelling narrative that resonates with the admissions committee and helps you stand out in the application process.

The Personal Interest Questions

The University of California does not accept the personal statement; instead, it asks applicants to write four shorter essays. Unlike the personal statement, the personal insight questions[128] do not assess your writing abilities but seek straightforward responses. You must respond to four of the eight questions, each capped at 350 words. Your activities list is an excellent starting point for identifying potential topics.

Link each of the four essays to at least one of the thirteen criteria of the UC's comprehensive review and ensure that the four prompts cover unique aspects of your life. Since all questions are considered equally, you should select the prompts you feel you can most compellingly answer. In your response, focus on content over style, as UC admissions readers

For the UCs:
Tell, don't show!

Chapter 10— Tips for Writing Your Essays

are looking for facts and genuine insight, not literary merit. Consider the PIQs as a written interview with an admissions officer and answer like you would in a real conversation.

Respond to the PIQs in three steps: First, introduce the idea without any fluff, impressionistic writing, or overarching themes. Next, answer all parts of the question and give specific examples. Third, describe how the experience has influenced you and connect the examples you outlined in step two to the results you explain in the third step. In this part, you address the 'so what?' question and convey the impact of your examples. Do not waste words by showcasing your elaborate use of literary devices; answer the question in a straightforward manner and tie your examples to your main ideas to illustrate the impact on your life.

- Present an idea
- Answer the prompt
- Share the impact: So what?

For questions related to academic subjects, connect your interests with your intended major or career paths. Explain how your passion for a subject has motivated you to seek further knowledge both inside and outside the classroom. The 'additional insights' question is a chance to mention anything that provides further context to your application, such as clarifications or significant aspects of your life that have not been covered elsewhere. As the UCs do not request or read letters of recommendation, answering this particular question allows you to provide additional context to your application if needed.

The UCs do not assess your writing skills

The 'Why Us?' Essay

Many colleges, including MIT, Rice, Yale, and Brown, require supplemental essays, specifically the popular prompt, 'Why us?'. Although it appears straightforward, this question demands more than merely listing your reasons for liking the college. Think of the essay as explaining a mutual match: How do the college's offerings complement your goals, and how will you contribute to the college community?

The 'Why us?' essay is not about writing what you like about the college; it's about establishing a personal connection with the college. This means aligning exciting aspects of its program with your interests and aspirations. Think of it as a mutual match: why are you and

> Why are you and the college the perfect match?

the college the perfect fit? By crafting a thoughtful, well-researched response, you can demonstrate your genuine interest and depth of your understanding of what the college offers. Remember, this essay is your opportunity to show the admissions officers why their institution needs you as much as you need them.

> Don't refer to location, ranking, reputation, or weather

If you have not done so already, take a moment to reflect on your academic interests, career ambitions, and what you hope to achieve through your college education. Next, dive deep into the college's website, focusing on specific programs, courses, extracurriculars, and unique opportunities that resonate with your goals. Consider reaching out to current students or admissions representatives for insider tips and using resources like the

Chapter 10— Tips for Writing Your Essays

Fiske Guide to Colleges and *niche.com* to get different perspectives and student reviews. In your response, highlight aspects of the college that are particularly appealing to you and not widely available at other institutions. This could include specialized academic programs, unique research opportunities, specific clubs, or community service initiatives that align with your interests.

While it is important to explain why the college is a perfect fit for you, it is equally crucial to discuss how you plan to contribute to the campus community. Outline how you will add value to the college through leadership roles, community service, or collaborative projects. Discuss between one to three specific goals you pursue and how the college's unique offerings support each goal. Dedicate a paragraph to each goal, weaving in detailed examples of courses, programs, and extracurricular activities offered at the college. Conclude by reiterating how the college will help you achieve your long-term goals and how you will enrich the campus community.

> Map specific aspects of a college with your goals

Personalizing your essay to each college and paying attention to details is crucial. Minor errors like a misspelled mascot or the wrong team colors can undermine your essay's credibility or suggest that you are not attentive to details. Resist the temptation to recycle a response you wrote for a different institution. If you can swap out the name of one college for a different one without having to change the rest of your essay, it is a telltale sign that your response is too generic. Remember, the more specific and tailored your response, the better.

> Do not recycle this essay

Chapter 11 – Application Strategies

You have worked hard inside and outside the classroom and crafted your best application. Now, it is time to identify the colleges you want to apply to. With over 4,000 different institutions in the United States, how do you go about sifting through them and finding the ones that fit you best? While there are many ways to identify colleges that are a good match for your unique situation, we suggest a Four Step approach.

Step 1: Identify Your Needs and Wants

While many can rattle off well-known and prestigious American colleges, a brand name does not guarantee that a particular institution is a good fit for you. Instead, you must identify those colleges that are a good match for your specific circumstances. At the right college, you will thrive academically, socially, and personally.

To identify these 'best fit' colleges, you must step back, introspect, and honestly assess your individual preferences and needs.

Key questions to assess your needs and wants:

- → What is your or your family's budget?
- → What academic interests, programs, and potential major(s) would you like to pursue?

- Do you prefer an urban, suburban, or rural setting? How important is the college's proximity to home, an airport, or potential job opportunities?
- What campus atmosphere and social environment are you looking for? Big sports teams? Music or arts communities? Fraternity or sorority (aka Greek life)?
- Do you have any political, religious, or other general preferences for the college or its location?
- What kind of college community are you looking for? Are you okay with a suitcase or a commuter college where many students go home for the weekend or after classes?
- How do you learn best? Do you prefer smaller classes where you can interact closely with professors, or are you comfortable in larger lecture settings? Are you looking for hands-on learning?
- How important are the residential facilities or guaranteed on-campus housing to you? Do you prefer apartment-style living, dorms, or off-campus housing? Do you prefer a single room without roommates?
- Do you want to pursue research, internships, or study abroad programs?
- How important is a college's prestige to you?
- What kind of academic culture do you prefer? Collaborative? Competitive?
- Do you plan to join specific clubs, organizations, or sports teams?
- How important is campus safety to you (and your family)?
- Do you have any preferences on climate? Can you deal with extremely hot or cold weather?
- What are your expectations for a diverse student body? How important is it to you to meet students from a similar background?

→ What kind of support infrastructure will you need? Financial aid? Mental health resources? Visa sponsoring? Counseling? Tutoring? Transfer counseling or career planning?

→ This question is worth repeating: What is your or your family's budget? How will you finance your college experience? Will you need a part-time job?

Step 2: Explore Your Options

Once you better understand your preferences and constraints, it is time to start your search and draft a preliminary list of potential colleges. Remember, this is an iterative process that may take longer than anticipated. As you learn more about each school and reflect on your priorities, you will likely add or remove colleges from your list and maybe even reconsider some of your criteria. Remain open-minded when discovering new schools; sometimes, the best fit may be a college you have never heard of and only found by chance. In this exploratory phase, you aim to identify schools you are excited to apply to and would be happy to attend.

Bird's-eye view:

-Big Future
-niche.com
-collegevine.com
-College Confidential
-Fiske Guide to Colleges

You can use various resources to identify colleges that fit your criteria and priorities. Start with a high-level scan of the college landscape to find potential candidates and maintain a spreadsheet mapping your criteria with potential colleges. This helps you create a list of possible colleges

Chapter 11 – Application Strategies

you want to research more thoroughly. Websites such as *niche.com*, *collegevine.com*, *collegeconfidential.com*, the College Board's Big Future website[129], Princeton Review[130], and the College Navigator[131] provide online tools for researching colleges based on various factors like location, size, majors, and campus life. If you would rather peruse a printed book, buy or rent the latest edition of the bestselling *Fiske Guide to Colleges*[132].

Once you have a preliminary list of colleges that may fit your criteria, it is time to dive into the specifics. Visit the official college websites to learn more about their academic programs, faculty credentials, extracurricular opportunities, campus amenities, and admission requirements. In addition, use the school's Common Data Sets and the information available in the Common App to better understand their demographics, admissions requirements, and deadlines. For instance, you can use the admissions statistics in the CDS to gauge your acceptance chances and help you create a balanced list. If a college of interest has a low acceptance rate, consider adding more safety schools to your list.

Research each potential college to build your list

But do not stop there. Attend in-person and virtual college fairs and regional events organized by your high school or directly by a college. This allows you to speak with admission representatives, ask questions, and get a feel for the college's atmosphere. If possible, attend in-person campus tours or tour the facilities independently to get a glimpse of the campus and its vibe. While there, interact with current students and faculty to gain insights into the academic and social life at the college. Since the pandemic, most colleges offer virtual tours and online information sessions, which are especially helpful if you cannot visit in person. Websites like *CampusTours.com* aggregate virtual tours of many campuses worldwide, and you can find unofficial tours by enrolled students on *YouTube*, giving firsthand accounts of their college life. Remember to view official tours, marketing materials, and unofficial videos critically; official presentations aim to promote the institution, whereas unofficial content may only reflect the experiences of some students.

Questions to ask an admissions officer or tour guide:

→ What is your favorite tradition at your college?
→ How hard is it to get the classes you want?
→ Do you guarantee housing for first-year students, potentially beyond the first year? Do you help finding off-campus housing?
→ What is the student-to-faculty ratio?
→ Do you provide smaller, more interactive discussion sessions alongside your larger lectures?
→ Do professors or graduate teaching assistants teach the classes ?
→ How easy is it for undergraduate students to participate in research or work in a lab?
→ Do professors hold regular office hours?
→ How many classes do first-year students usually take?
→ On average, how many years does it take to graduate?
→ What are your GE (general education) requirements?
→ How often do students meet their academic advisors?
→ How easy or hard is it to change one's major?
→ What resources do you have for students struggling academically?
→ What advice would you offer to someone either applying to your college or about to begin their first year?

Email the admissions office any questions about programs of interest or if you would like general application advice. Your assigned regional officer will respond, allowing you to start a dialogue, demonstrate your interest, and avoid a stealth application. In addition, follow colleges on social media and browse student forums to get a sense of the community and current topics of interest among students.

Review college brochures, viewbooks, and other marketing materials you find online or receive by mail. You may get some insights into a college's institutional priorities by how it presents itself to prospective students. However, do not rely solely on these materials. Discuss your college list with your high school counselor and parents. Reach out to people who attend or have graduated from the colleges on your list, as their personal experiences can provide insights that you may not find in official publications. By combining these strategies and resources, you can develop a well-informed list of colleges that align with your academic goals and personal preferences. Remember, the key is to find schools where you can thrive academically and socially.

> Keep track of details found via college websites, CDS, marketing material, campus tours, and college fairs

Step 3: Build a Balanced Shortlist

During the exploratory phase, you have compiled an extensive list of colleges that may be a good fit. In fact, your preliminary list most likely exceeds the number of colleges you can possibly apply to. In the next step, you will condense your preliminary list into a shorter, more manageable one, allowing you to effectively use your available resources – time, energy, and money.

By limiting the number of colleges you apply to, you can spend more time on each application, allowing you to customize them to meet the specific requirements of each college. Applying to fewer colleges with a strong, high-quality application may yield better results than spreading yourself thin with superficial applications to numerous colleges. These days, most applicants apply to ten to twelve different colleges. In this stage, applicants usually sort potential colleges into three major categories based on their admission chances. These categories are safety schools, where you are likely to be accepted; target schools, where you have a solid chance; and reach schools, where the competition is high and your odds of getting in are low. A balanced college list typically includes three to four schools in each category. This approach increases your chances of admission and provides a range of options.

> Diversify your shortlist with 3 to 4 reach, target, and safety schools

A reach school is a college where the applicant's academic profile is typically below the average admitted student. Highly selective colleges with an admission rate under 20% also fall in this category. Unless the applicant has a unique hook, like being a legacy or a recruited athlete, all Ivies and highly selective colleges like MIT or Stanford are reach schools for everyone. Students who apply exclusively to these schools risk not receiving any acceptances. You can avoid this by casting a wide net and

> Colleges with acceptance rates lower than 20% are reach schools for all applicants

including colleges that are more likely to admit you: your target and safety schools.

In a target school, your profile aligns closely with those of previously admitted students, increasing the likelihood of acceptance. For instance, your GPA and standardized test scores typically fall within the 50th to 75th percentile of past admissions. Use the CDS to assess the competitiveness of your profile, as this helps you to classify the colleges on your shortlist. However, with the recent explosion of applications and an increased emphasis on yield management, many qualified applicants surprisingly receive rejections from institutions they consider targets. To minimize this risk and alleviate the stress of the application process, you need a safety net.

Safety schools are colleges where you are likely to be admitted, as your academic profile is well above their admissions statistics. Your GPA and test scores will be in the top quartile of past admissions, making you a desirable candidate. Apply to multiple safety schools; most applicants have at least four safeties on their shortlist. If you plan to major in a highly popular field like computer science or engineering, consider adding more than four safety schools. Select colleges you would be happy to attend, and do not overlook them simply because they may not be widely recognized. Safety colleges may provide significant merit-based scholarships to strong applicants, potentially making them more affordable than target or reach schools.

> Include colleges with rolling admissions and guaranteed admit programs

Remember that even at safety schools, admission is not guaranteed, as they may practice yield protection, have distinct institutional priorities, or get too many applications in a particular field. Including colleges with rolling admissions or guaranteed admit programs can significantly reduce stress and result in better outcomes. If finances are a consideration, apply to more safety schools, as they are more likely to provide merit-based aid than your target or reach schools.

> As you matched them with your needs, all colleges on your shortlist are a good fit – including your safety schools

Given that you have crafted your shortlist to match your needs and wants, all colleges, including your safeties, are a good fit for you! International students should also consider a college's ability to sponsor a student visa and the overall number of international students on campus. The Department of Homeland Security[133] keeps a database of all visa-sponsoring colleges, and the school's CDS profile will indicate its percentage of enrolled international students.

Step 4: Check for Affordability

By now, you have crafted a diverse list of good-fit colleges based on your specific circumstances and feel ready to apply. However, before you hit the 'submit' button, there is one last critical step – ensure that you can afford to attend. At

> CoA: tuition, room & board, and other incidentals without travel cost

Chapter 11 – Application Strategies

some private colleges, like Harvard or Stanford, the total cost of attendance surpasses $80,000 per year, amounting to over $320,000 for a four-year degree. Recently, Vanderbilt University and the University of Southern California have made national headlines by increasing their total cost to nearly $100,000 per year. The cost of obtaining an undergraduate degree from one of these institutions can be equivalent to purchasing a single-family home. This heavy price tag underscores the importance of verifying that you can cover all expenses before applying. By focusing on financially feasible options, you direct your efforts toward applications that are a good fit in all aspects – academically, socially, and financially.

When creating your shortlist, note whether a college considers your ability to pay. Some colleges do not take an applicant's financial situation into account when making admission decisions. Applying to these need-blind colleges ensures that your financial need does not negatively impact your chances of acceptance. While these schools admit students regardless of their financial situation, being need-blind does not guarantee that the college will meet 100% of your demonstrated financial need. You may be accepted, but the college may not provide enough financial aid to cover all costs. Yet, many wealthy need-blind institutions are known for offering generous financial aid packages for domestic students. As an international student, always check if policies apply to non-residents.

> Need-blind colleges do not consider financial need in admission decisions

Colleges meeting 100% of an applicant's demonstrated need provide enough financial aid and loans to cover the cost of attendance. Demonstrated financial need refers to the difference between the cost of attendance and the expected family contribution. Yet, what the college considers demonstrated financial need may differ from what your family deems affordable. Always run the college's Net Price Calculator on their website to understand how much a college expects you to contribute.

> Colleges meeting 100% of demonstrated need provide sufficient aid & loans to cover all cost

Some institutions, such as Williams College and Swarthmore College, went one step further and eliminated the need to take out student loans. Colleges with no-loan policies award financial aid exclusively through grants and scholarships that do not need to be repaid. Student loans are borrowed money that a student or their parents must repay with accrued interest. Grants are often awarded based on a student's financial need, whereas scholarships are typically merit-based and awarded for academic or athletic achievements.

> Most colleges are need-aware and consider financial need in decisions

Although a few institutions can offer substantial financial aid due to their large endowments, most American colleges lack the resources to provide such generous assistance. To ensure their long-term financial stability, need-aware colleges factor in the financial means of their applicants. This does not mean that you will be rejected if you require financial aid, but your financial need will be one of the decision factors. If you cannot cover all college costs

Chapter 11 – Application Strategies

out of pocket, prioritize colleges that commit to meeting 100% of your demonstrated financial need, ideally without taking out loans.

In an ideal combination, a college is need-blind in its admissions process, implements no-loan policies, and commits to meeting 100% of a student's demonstrated financial need. If you require financial assistance or scholarships, research the application processes and deadlines of these options. As an international student, try to identify colleges that offer above-average financial aid packages. For example, Wesleyan University and Wellesley College offer international students over $80,000 in dedicated scholarships[134], demonstrating their commitment to supporting global education.

The ideal college is need-blind and meets 100% of demonstrated need without loans

The Net Price Calculator on a college's website helps you understand the financial implications of attending. You receive a personalized estimate of what you can expect to pay by inputting your financial data. The NPC considers all costs, such as tuition, room and board, books, and other expenses, and subtracts any grants or scholarships, giving you the college's net price. This online calculator lets you assess the affordability of each prospective college and compare costs across all schools on your shortlist. You can access a college's NPC by searching the college's name and 'net price calculator' or through the central interface of the Department of Education[135].

Run the Net Price Calculator for each prospective college before applying

If your shortlist needs more affordable options, add more safety schools, as they are more likely to award merit-based scholarships than target or reach schools. 2+2 programs are another option to explore, as they can significantly reduce your overall cost of college. These programs allow you to begin your studies at a more affordable community college and transfer to a four-year institution after two years. You can find more information on financing your college education in the next chapter.

Additional Tactics

In addition to the suggested Four-Step strategy, you can employ the following tactics to stay on track with your applications and improve your applicant profile.

Organize Your College Applications

Since college admissions is a highly complex process with many moving parts, keeping track of the wealth of data, including application requirements, costs, and deadlines, is critical. After doing multiple campus tours and researching various programs online, I needed help remembering all the details. Yet, these details may become essential when writing the 'Why Us?' essay or deciding between two college offers at decision time.

==Get organized so you don't miss a deadline==

In addition, being well organized ensures that you submit your applications well before their deadlines and allows you to compare acceptance offers when they roll in. You can choose from several apps and digital tools to organize your application process.

Chapter 11 – Application Strategies

Helpful apps to organize your college applications:

→ *Google Sheets* and *Microsoft Excel* create customizable spreadsheets tracking various aspects of your college applications. You can access these tools from anywhere and share them with parents or counselors for input and advice.

→ *Trello* uses a system of boards, lists, and cards to help you organize tasks and information visually. You can create a board for each college and list items like application tasks, essays, recommendation letters, and deadlines. You can attach files, set reminders, and collaborate with your school counselor, independent college counselor, and parents.

→ *Evernote* lets you create digital notebooks for different colleges, such as essay drafts, financial aid information, or college visit notes.

→ While primarily an application platform, the *Common App* also offers tools to manage and track your applications to multiple institutions through one portal. It provides a centralized place to monitor each school's deadlines, submission statuses, and other requirements.

→ The application portal *SCOIR* also offers free online college planning tools.

→ Used by many American high schools, *Naviance* is a college and career readiness platform that allows you to research colleges, track application deadlines, and manage documents like transcripts and recommendation letters. It also provides college suggestions based on your profile. Naviance is well-known for its scattergrams, which chart the admission outcomes of previous students from the same high school, letting you gauge your acceptance chances.

→ Another free option is *Notion*, an all-in-one workspace where you can write, plan, collaborate, and organize. You can use it to create a comprehensive database of colleges, application requirements, deadlines, and personal notes.

→ Some independent college counselors work with *CollegePlannerPro*, a paid app designed to manage college lists, compare colleges, track application components, and meet deadlines.

Pick the app that works best for you, whether you prefer visual boards, detailed spreadsheets, comprehensive databases, or a combination of these methods. Next, map all potential colleges with your criteria based on your circumstances and priorities. Begin with the needs and wants you identified in Step 1 as a foundation of your research and analysis. Make sure to cover all your limitations, particularly your family's budget. Nothing is more heartbreaking than being admitted but unable to afford a college. Include any other relevant aspects specific to your situation; this will allow you to compare potential colleges during and after the application process when determining which institution to attend. You can utilize a particular detail in the 'Why Us?' essay or during an interview with an admissions officer to bolster your argument of being the ideal candidate.

> Keep track of all details as they may be critical for essays and when deciding for a college

This tracker becomes your dynamic, personalized tool for determining how well a particular college matches your preferences and specific needs. Being organized also ensures that you submit your applications and necessary materials by the deadlines. Remember there is no leeway to submit your application on time. The application tracker is particularly valuable during decision-making times.

Possible elements to include in your application tracker:

- ☐ Your **non-negotiable** factors (your 'needs' from Step 1)
- ☐ Your **desirable attributes** (your 'wants' from Step 1)
- ☐ **SEVP-approved** college to sponsor F-1 student visa
- ☐ Total **cost of attending,** including tuition, fees, and room and board. Include the sticker price and the net price from the Net Price Calculator
- ☐ Your **family's budget**
- ☐ **Financial need policies:** need-blind; need-aware; meets 100% of demonstrated need; loan-free policy
- ☐ **Distance from home**, including your willingness to travel, financial implications of getting to and from college, nearest (international) airport, and the availability of direct or connecting flights to your hometown
- ☐ **Size:** Faculty and students, including faculty-to-student ratio
- ☐ **Location** (U.S. state and nearest large city) – consider political climate, social, professional, and recreational opportunities. Include geographic climate if you have preferences.
- ☐ **Type of college**: research university, small liberal arts college, public or private institution, commuter college, party school
- ☐ **Campus setting**: urban, rural, or suburban
- ☐ **Other opportunities**: Specific major-related programs, research, projects, study abroad, internships
- ☐ **Social scene**: Clubs, sports, Greek life: sororities, fraternities (Note: Attending a school with prevalent Greek life without the intention to join may constrain your options for social interactions)
- ☐ **Demonstrated interest** considered?

MISSION: ACCEPTED!

- ☐ **Admission rates** by/ for: application program (ED, EA, RD); major (impacted vs. less popular ones); international or transfer students
- ☐ Percentage of **international students**
- ☐ **Legacy admissions**
- ☐ **Housing:** traditional dorms vs. apartment-style housing; single, double, triple occupancy; length of guaranteed housing; availability and cost of off-campus housing
- ☐ **Application deadlines** by decision plan: ED, EA, REA, RD (Note: Colleges do not accept late applications; all deadlines are set according to the local U.S. time zone of the respective college)
- ☐ **Financial aid applications**: FAFSA or CSS Profile accepted, deadlines
- ☐ **Testing policies**: SAT or ACT required; test-optional; test-flexible (SAT, ACT, AP, or IB), test-optional; test-blind
- ☐ **Language proficiency** tests and minimum scores: TOEFL, IELTS, Duo Lingo
- ☐ **AP or IB credits**: Which courses? Number of credits granted
- ☐ Number and prompts of **supplemental essays** and questions
- ☐ **Supplemental submissions**: Portfolios; artistic supplements; videos; live auditions
- ☐ **Letters of recommendation**: how many are required or recommended; type of recommender (teacher, counselor, outside recommender)
- ☐ **Honors programs**
- ☐ **Interviews:** required; recommended; not available; deadlines to request an optional interview
- ☐ **Academic profiles**: Track the 50th and 75th percentile of GPA, SAT, and ACT in the CDS
- ☐ **Application fees**

Chapter 11 – Application Strategies

- ☐ **Freshman year retention**[2] and **4-year graduation rates**[3] as indicators of student satisfaction and success
- ☐ Availability of **merit-based scholarships**; percentage of students receiving merit aid
- ☐ **Policies for international students**
- ☐ **Impacted majors:** which majors are impacted; policies to switch into impacted majors later?
- ☐ **Demographic makeup** (gender, race, housed vs. commuting students, international students, etc.)
- ☐ **Commitment date** (if different from the standard May 1)
- ☐ **Religious affiliation**
- ☐ **Co-ed** versus male-/female-only
- ☐ **Safety**: campus safety[136]; safety of the surrounding city[137]
- ☐ **Prestige and ranking**

Strategic Choice of Majors

While some applicants are determined to pursue one particular major or academic field, others have a broad range of interests and consider multiple unrelated majors. For those students who are flexible in their potential field of study, it can be a powerful strategy to apply to different colleges with different majors. When strategically choosing a major for

---

[2] Freshman year retention is the percentage of first-year students who continue their studies at the same institution for their second year. It is often considered an indicator of student satisfaction.

[3] The 4-year graduation rate measures the percentage of students who complete their undergraduate degree within four years of enrolling at a college. It assesses how effective a college is in enabling students to achieve their academic goals within the expected timeframe.

college admissions, you can employ several tactics to enhance your chances of acceptance, especially when targeting impacted majors or considering very uncommon ones.

Impacted Majors

Impacted majors, also known as capped, selective, screened, or high-demand majors, are programs that attract significantly more applicants than there are available spots. Fields like computer science, engineering, nursing, and business are impacted at most colleges. These majors usually have significantly higher admission standards and more competition during admissions. To manage the high volume of applications, numerous colleges directly admit students into impacted majors. In direct admission systems, applicants must declare their major at the time of their initial application. Once they are admitted directly into a capped major, students are guaranteed a place in that program, but switching into these programs later can be extremely difficult, if not impossible. In addition, applicants for highly popular majors usually face higher admission standards due to the limited space and high demand.

> Impacted majors have more applicants than spots

> If not directly admitted as a first-year student, it is difficult to change into an impacted major later

Usually, admission rates for impacted majors are significantly lower than the overall acceptance rate of a college. For example, UC Davis admits about 10% of applicants into its Computer Science program[138] compared to its general admission rate of 37%. When planning to apply to an impacted major, it is essential to understand the prerequisites and admission requirements well before applying. Some programs may require specific math, computer, or science classes, such as AP Biology, AP Computer Science A, or AP Calculus B/C.

> Acceptance rates for impacted majors are lower

To be a competitive applicant for an impacted major, you need excellent grades in coursework relevant to your prospective major and demonstrate your commitment through extracurricular activities such as internships or a passion project. Cast a wide net and apply to a diverse range of colleges with varying levels of selectivity for your intended major. In addition, include plenty of safety schools where your desired program is less constrained. When considering a capped major, your shortlist should include more safety schools than when applying to an uncapped one. For the most popular majors, such as computer science, the concept of safety schools may not even apply.

Alternate Majors

Many colleges allow applicants to choose an alternate major in case they are not admitted to their first choice. Considering alternate majors is an additional strategy to improve your chances of admission. Exploring related majors that may have lower demand but still align with your interests and career goals can be a strategic move.

> Selecting an alternate major may increase your admission chances

For example, data science and machine learning have emerged as popular alternatives to the highly impacted field of computer science.

Considering alternate majors broadens your options and increases your chances of acceptance, making it a valuable strategy in your college application process. However, selecting an alternate major should not be viewed as a backdoor strategy for entering a more selective program, as most colleges will not permit students to switch to a competitive major if they were not initially admitted into that program. Be sure that you would be satisfied completing your degree in the alternate major if accepted under the secondary choice.

Uncommon Majors, Double Majoring

Applying for an uncommon major can also be a strategic choice, as these programs may have fewer applicants, potentially increasing your chances of acceptance. Examples of unusual majors include comic art, adventure education, fermentation science, or amusement park engineering.

Yet, applying to an uncommon major is not just about potentially increasing your chances of admission. Selecting a less popular major can open doors to unique opportunities. It can distinguish you in the admissions process, as admissions officers often look for a diverse incoming class with a wide range of interests and skills. Uncommon majors often have smaller class sizes, allowing for more personalized attention from professors and more intimate class discussions. Additionally, students may find unique opportunities for research, internships, and hands-on experiences, which can provide a competitive edge when entering the job market or applying for graduate programs.

> Consider applying to an uncommon major

Pursuing a double major, combining an uncommon field with a more traditional one, or opting for a major-minor combination can also enhance your opportunities in the workforce. While minors are not mandatory, they can enrich your educational experience and bolster your profile in the job market.

Applying Undecided

For students needing more time to decide what they want to major in, some colleges allow you to apply with the major 'undecided' or 'undeclared.' These exploratory programs allow students to explore coursework before deciding on a major after one or two years. Applying undecided can be a strategic choice if you have multiple areas of interest or are just not ready yet to commit to a specific major.

> Applying undecided may limit your major choices later

Some colleges allow undeclared students to choose any major after their exploratory studies; others limit the choice of major to a particular program or college, such as, for example, their College of Letters and Arts.

However, most colleges do not allow undecided students to transfer to an impacted major later, particularly if they use a direct admit program. It is very unlikely to be able to switch to computer science or the college of engineering as an undecided student! Another drawback is that undeclared students typically receive later time slots for course enrollment for the next term. This lower enrollment priority could result in difficulty securing required classes, potentially extending the time needed to graduate. If you apply without declaring a major, you may not be able to graduate within four years. Make sure you understand all potential downsides before applying to a college without declaring a specific major.

Get Expert Help

School Counselors

Most American high schools have dedicated staff members guiding students from freshman to senior year. These school or college counselors help navigate the plethora of academic courses and the complexities of college applications. In addition, they assist the students in building their college lists, provide feedback on essays, send school profiles and transcripts to colleges, and write and coordinate letters of recommendation.

-School counselors
-IECs
-Essay coaches
-Test prep & tutors
-Online resources

With these responsibilities, school counselors are an important support system for students throughout their high school years, particularly during college admissions. Direct access to an experienced and knowledgeable guidance counselor is an asset for every high school student. Research has shown that high school juniors with regular one-on-one meetings with their school counselor are more than three times as likely to attend college and twice as likely to enroll in a bachelor's program[139]. This underscores the significant impact of personalized guidance on students' aspirations and college enrollment.

School counselors advise on course selection and support college applications

However, the availability of resources varies greatly, with more affluent schools being able to fund more dedicated staff, providing higher levels of support. Not only is there a general shortage of school counselors nationwide, but most counselors are overwhelmed with large caseloads and burdened with administrative tasks. While the National Association for College Admission Counseling recommends 250 students per full-time counselor, the national average is 430, almost double the recommendation[140].

> Most school counselors have high caseloads, preventing individual support

Even with the recommended ratio of 1:250, a school counselor responsible for hundreds of students is unlikely to offer individualized support and guidance beyond administrative tasks such as submitting transcripts and letters of recommendation. Public high school counselors spend only 18% of their time on personalized college counseling, compared to 31% at private high schools[141]. While school counselors provide the best support they can, they often do not have the capacity or expertise to guide each student individually.

Independent Educational Consultants

With high school counselors stretched so thin, it is no surprise that many affluent American families hire independent educational consultants to support them through the ever-changing and complex college admissions process. IECs provide

> Many families hire independent college counselors

access to valuable resources and insider knowledge as they usually have extensive networks and firsthand experience with various colleges.

Based on their insights into specific programs, campus cultures, and admission trends, they can suggest great-fit colleges, help craft a compelling narrative in a student's essays, or prepare them for admissions interviews. IECs typically have a background in education or professional experience in areas such as counseling or higher education administration. Many worked as admissions officers before becoming independent consultants.

When choosing an IEC, seek counselors with certifications from respected professional organizations like the NACAC[142] or IECA[143]. These credentials demonstrate their commitment to upholding ethical standards and staying informed about industry developments. Many independent counselors operate on multi-year contracts, supporting families long-term as they navigate the college admissions process. Make sure that the consultant's pricing model, whether all-inclusive or hourly billing, aligns with your family's budget.

> Consider NACAC- or IECA-accredited counselors

Essay Coaches

Some families hire a consultant specialized in crafting compelling essays. Essay coaches are often professional writers or editors and help identify meaningful and authentic narratives that capture a student's unique perspective. While essay coaches do not write the essays for the students, they provide feedback on essay drafts, offer suggestions for improvements, and assist with the essay's organization and focus. This way, they ensure that each essay is impactful and supports the overall narrative of the application.

Test Preparation Companies

Test preparatory companies help students achieve their target scores on standardized tests such as the SAT, ACT, or AP exams. They provide review courses that cover the content and format of standardized tests, teach test-taking strategies, and execute proctored practice tests. Beyond preparing for exams, they instill essential study habits, time management skills, and exam strategies that can serve students throughout their academic and professional lives. Test prep consultants usually offer personalized tutoring services in one-on-one or small group settings to identify areas of weakness and develop customized study plans. They also provide tools to monitor test performance, such as online practice tests, diagnostic assessments, and score reports that provide detailed feedback on a student's strengths and areas for improvement.

> Test preparatory companies offer tutoring to improve SAT, ACT, or AP scores

Free Online Resources

While the services of college and test prep consultants may enhance a student's chances of admission, not everyone can afford these services. However, numerous free resources are available today without the hefty price tag of external consultants. These resources assist students in various aspects of the college admissions process, ensuring that professional support is accessible to all.

Free professional resources:

→ ACT Academy[144] offers test prep for the ACT
→ AXS Companion[145] offers detailed instructions and videos to fill out the CommonApp
→ College Board offers the Bluebook app to practice for the digital SAT[146]
→ College Possible[147] offers free mentoring programs
→ College Advising Corps[148] connects students with admissions counselors
→ Get Schooled[149] offers essay review and advising via text messages
→ Khan Academy[150] offers personalized practice tools for the ACT, SAT, and AP exams
→ Revision Learning[151] and the College Essay Guy[152] offer tools for writing college essays

Transfer Students

Transferring from a community college to a 4-year institution can be another strategic choice. Community colleges typically offer lower tuition rates, making them an attractive alternative for students seeking to save money on their undergraduate education. After the transfer, a student's diploma and academic credentials will reflect the degree program and institution where they completed their coursework; this means that a student who transferred from a

Receive your diploma from the 4-year institution

Chapter 11 – Application Strategies

community college to UC Berkeley will receive the same diploma as a student who enrolled at UCB as a freshman!

One of the main benefits is the ability to bring credits earned at the community college to the new institution, allowing them to obtain their bachelor's degree after two additional years. Students enrolled at a four-year college can also transfer to a different institution for their sophomore or junior year if they believe the other institution is a better fit. When planning your transfer, work closely with the academic advisors and transfer services office at the prospective college to inquire about their credit transfer policies. Your advisor helps you understand which credits can be transferred to your new program. Credits may be granted for pre-approved courses or based on the course's syllabus and your grades.

Transfer your GE and 'lower division' coursework

Find UC-approved transfer courses at assist.org

Many public universities have established transfer agreements with in-state community colleges to encourage social and academic mobility. These agreements outline dedicated pathways to completing degree requirements and credit transfers from the community college to the 4-year university. For example, transfer agreement programs allow eligible students from a California community college to get guaranteed or preferential admission to participating UC campuses. These mutual agreements ensure a smooth transfer of academic credits and may increase your chances of admission to your desired four-year college; most transfer students admitted to a

University of California campus come from a California community college.

Participating UCs accept up to 70 semester or 104 quarter credit units[153] for coursework from a California community college or another 4-year institution. At the same time, community college students must complete a minimum of 60 semester or 90 quarter units to be eligible for transfer[154]. To apply, transfer students must complete a formal application, including academic transcripts, letters of recommendation from college professors, and supplemental essays.

Transfer agreements ensure smooth course transfers

Potential Drawbacks

However, transferring colleges comes with its own set of challenges. A common pitfall results from the difference in term systems. While some community colleges follow the quarter system, many four-year institutions use the semester system. As quarter courses may cover less content, colleges with the semester system often restrict acceptance of coursework completed under the quarter system. In addition, admissions criteria may be more stringent for transfer students, with some colleges imposing higher GPA requirements than for first-year applicants.

Research transfer policies well in advance

Another possible drawback of transferring to a new institution involves financial aid. Some colleges allocate most of their financial aid funds to first-year students, leaving only a small portion to transfer students. Consequently, transfer students should explore available financial aid

Chapter 11 – Application Strategies

and scholarship options, as these packages may vary depending on the policies of the new institution.

Another pitfall is the fact that, occasionally, high school graduates can inadvertently transition into transfer students. Enrolling in any post-secondary institution following high school prompts admissions offices to classify you as a transfer student. Instead of your high school GPA, they will assess your application based on your performance in your college classes. Keep this in mind if you intend to take a gap year and plan to enroll in just a few college courses to occupy your time. Regardless of the extent of your enrollment, once you join any college program, you assume the status of a transfer student – even if you took just one class!

> Enrolling in any college post-high school forfeits first-year status

Transfer students may also face different acceptance rates compared to freshmen applicants. Some colleges have higher acceptance rates for transfer students, particularly those with established transfer agreements, whereas others may maintain more competitive admission standards. Consult a college's website and Common Data Set to gain insight into its admission rates and transfer requirements.

Chapter 12 — Paying for College

While some countries offer free university education, American colleges charge tuition to cover the cost of instruction and educational services. Students are also responsible for accommodation, meal plans, textbooks, and various fees. Let us examine the total expenses of studying in the U.S. and discuss options for covering these costs.

Cost of Attendance

Most colleges outline on their websites what prospective students can expect to pay for one academic year. The cost of attendance at some colleges can reach $100,000 per year, which, over the course of a four-year degree, adds up to the equivalent of purchasing a single-family home. Generally, CoA includes tuition, fees, room and board, books and supplies, health insurance, transportation, and sometimes personal expenses. Keep in mind that travel costs are not included. When compiling your college list, you must consider the total cost of attendance plus any travel costs, as this reflects your overall financial commitment.

> Cost of attendance can be up to $100,000 per year

By shortlisting colleges that are within your budget, you ensure that, if accepted, you can afford to attend them. Cost is likely a factor when

Chapter 12 – Paying for College

deciding between two or more colleges. Understanding your total expenses allows you to budget effectively and identify potential sources of financial aid, such as scholarships, grants, and loans.

Public institutions are generally more affordable than private ones, as they receive funding from the government and taxpayers, reducing the overall cost for students. To reflect that local families already contribute with tax payments, public colleges usually offer lower tuition rates for in-state residents than out-of-state or international students. Private colleges, which rely heavily on tuition revenue, generally have higher tuition rates and do not discriminate between in-state and out-of-state rates. The cost of operating a college campus can vary significantly depending on the geographical location, and urban colleges often have higher tuition rates than those in rural areas with lower overhead costs.

Tuition covers the cost of academic instruction and services

The largest contributor to the cost of attendance is tuition, which is the fee charged for attending academic classes, accessing the campus facilities, and receiving academic support. Private institutions frequently have higher tuition rates than public colleges. For the 2024/25 academic year, Yale's tuition[155] – without housing, food, or other expenses –exceeds $67,000, and the University of Southern California[156] charges over $69,000.

Despite the high costs of attending some selective colleges, many families are willing to pay a hefty premium for their perceived prestige and value. Nonetheless, with thousands of colleges across the United States, alternative pathways exist to get a college education.

Cost comparison between private and public institutions in 2024/25:

	University of Southern California[157] all students	University of California[158] in-state	University of California[158] out-of-state / international
Tuition	$69,904	$14,436	$48,636
Fees	$1,743	$1,800	$1,800
On-campus Housing and Meal Plan	$19,931	$19,200	$19,200
Health insurance	$3,000*	$3,000	$3,000
Books & Supplies	$1,200	$1,300	$1,300
Personal Expenses	$2,000	$2,000*	$2,000*
Transportation	$441	$2,500	$2,500
Cost of Attendance	**$98,219**	**$44,236**	**$78,436**

(*estimated)

On top of tuition, other expenses like room and board, fees, books and supplies, transportation, and health insurance contribute to the overall cost of attendance. At most colleges, health insurance coverage is mandatory, and some offer the option to purchase campus health insurance through their institution.

Research the total cost for each potential college on their website and use their Net Price Calculator to estimate your expected cost after merit and financial aid. Check if a college gives credit for AP or IB exams, as you may be able to skip some lower division and general education classes, potentially accelerating your time to graduation.

In addition, look at student graduation rates within four and six years. Not all students complete their degree within four years, and extending your studies will increase your total financial commitment. International students must add the cost of obtaining a student visa plus the travel cost to and from the U.S. to their home country.

> Use the NPC and graduation rate to estimate your total cost until graduation

Financing Your College Experience

Since the total expense of a U.S. college education can be comparable to buying a house, it is vital to plan this investment carefully. Few people would purchase a home without a thorough financial analysis or considering the potential return on their investment. Yet, some students commit to a college without prior cost analysis, basing their decision mainly on the college's prestige. The ongoing debate in the States about student loan forgiveness reflects the financial challenges many Americans encounter. They often take on loans without fully understanding or considering the long-term financial impact. Let us explore the various options for financing your

> Cost of attendance over four years may be equivalent to buying a house

college education, including savings plans, financial assistance, work-study programs, and student loans. Next, we will discuss possible strategies for negotiating any financial awards you receive.

529 College Savings Plans

Many American families start saving for their children's college education when the first baby is born. The U.S. government supports these efforts by providing tax-free savings plans. 529 college savings plans allow families to invest in mutual funds or exchange-traded funds using tax benefits. The earnings on these investments and withdrawals are tax-free as long as families use them for qualified education expenses. These expenses typically include tuition, fees, books, supplies, and, depending on the plan, room and board. Some plans allow for contributions from extended family and friends, making it a collaborative effort to save for education expenses.

> 529 college savings plans are tax-free

However, if funds are withdrawn for non-qualified expenses, the earnings portion of the withdrawal may be subject to income tax and a 10% penalty. 529 plans are designed for U.S. citizens or resident aliens, which means they are not accessible to international families. To finance their college education, international students must explore alternative options, such as private family funds, financial aid, student loans, and legal employment opportunities.

Chapter 12 – Paying for College

Types of Financial Aid

As colleges aim to make education accessible to all, they provide various types of financial assistance. They typically outline the financial aid they offer in the admissions letter or a separate document. Financial aid packages include information about the total costs of attending and any financial assistance, such as grants, scholarships, federal work-study programs, and loans.

Overview of different types of financial aid:

	Grants	Scholarships	Loans	Work-study
Based on	need	merit	personal finances	need
Eligibility criteria	– income – assets	– academics – athletics	–credit score – assets	– income – assets
Funded by	– government – college – foundations	– college – foundations	– government – banks	government
Repay?	no	no	yes, with interest	no
International students eligible?	no (federal)	depends	– no (federal) – depends (private)	no

At the same time, financial aid letters are notoriously difficult to read and interpret. As such, you should carefully review the letters and contact the office of financial assistance for clarification if needed. To help make sense of the information, you can create a spreadsheet to compare offers from different colleges. It is important to compare apples to apples, as some colleges may use inconsistent definitions or terms.

Verify that your financial aid is renewable for the following years

Make sure to confirm that your financial aid is renewable for subsequent years and what the requirements are for maintaining eligibility. To attract students to enroll, some colleges use a tactic called 'front-loading,' where they provide most of their institutional aid in the first year. However, this practice may leave students with an unpleasant surprise in the following years when they find out they receive significantly less financial aid than expected.

Various tools and resources are available to assist students in understanding their financial aid packages, such as the *Federal College Financing Plan*[159] and independent tools like the *Offer Letter Decoder*[160]. These resources provide annotated explanations of the contents of your financial aid letters. The timing of financial aid award letters varies depending on the college's policies and the student's application timeline. Private colleges tend to send offers earlier than public institutions, while community colleges may have even later timelines.

Financial Aid Applications

To be considered for need-based financial aid, you must disclose your family's financials. The U.S. government and colleges then determine how much financial assistance they offer you based on your situation. The most commonly used application for reporting family finances is

FAFSA, but some colleges request the family's financial data through the CSS Profile. Depending on the college, international students will use either the CSS Profile or ISFAA. Let us look at each application individually.

FAFSA

Many colleges and U.S. states use the Free Application for Federal Student Aid[161] to determine eligibility for both federal and institutional financial aid programs. This form is submitted online and needs to be completed annually. The application requests financial information such as household income, federal income tax returns, untaxed income, and records of family assets.

> FAFSA determines your federal aid and is often the basis for institutional need-based aid

Based on this data, the FAFSA calculates the Student Aid Index (formerly called 'Expected Family Contribution'). The SAI is the amount the government believes your family can contribute to your educational expenses and determines the type of federal aid you qualify for. In addition, colleges may use the SAI to determine the amount of institutional financial aid you may receive. The FAFSA application was overhauled for the 2024/25 season. However, instead of streamlining the process, the changes caused many technical issues, causing major delays in processing applications. Many students did not get their financial aid information before the decision day on May 1.

> Student Aid Index = amount the U.S. government believes your family can contribute

Three different FAFSA deadlines exist: First, colleges set their own deadlines, typically well before the academic year begins; check the college's financial aid webpage or contact their office to verify the deadlines. Second, your home state determines its own FAFSA deadline. Since U.S. states have limited funds, submitting your FAFSA promptly is crucial to securing government aid. Third, the U.S. Department of Education sets the federal deadline, marking the end of the academic year. The FAFSA form becomes unavailable after June 30. Submit your FAFSA form as soon as possible, as missing one of the deadlines could result in loss of financial assistance.

> Some colleges request two applications: FAFSA and CSS Profile

The CSS Profile

In addition to the standard FAFSA application, some selective colleges require applicants to complete a separate financial aid application to evaluate their need for institutional aid. While the FAFSA primarily determines eligibility for federal financial aid programs, some colleges also request the College Scholarship Service Profile[162] to assess a student's financial need and award their own institutional aid.

> Institutional aid may be awarded based on the CSS Profile

The CSS Profile collects more detailed financial details than the FAFSA. Unlike the free FAFSA form, the CSS Profile requires a processing fee;

Chapter 12 – Paying for College

the first CSS application costs $25 and each additional one $16. The CSS Profile deadline differs for each institution but typically falls between January 1 and March 31 for students applying through the regular decision process. As a U.S. citizen or permanent resident, fill out the FAFSA form to qualify for federal aid and the CSS Profile for non-federal aid from participating institutions. Some colleges may accept the CSS Profile from international students when evaluating their eligibility for financial aid.

ISFAA

With some exceptions[163], most foreign citizens do not qualify for FAFSA. However, many colleges will accept the CSS Profile or ask for a paper copy of the International Student Financial Aid Application. Like the CSS, the ISFAA collects detailed financial information about the student and their family's finances to assess their eligibility for institutional financial aid. International students may be required to submit the ISFAA along with other application materials when applying for financial aid at U.S. colleges. There is no fee to complete the ISFAA. If requested by a college, you must download the ISFAA form from their website and mail a paper copy of it.

> International students may use the CSS Profile and ISFAA

Comparison of financial aid applications:

	FAFSA	CSS	ISFAA
International students eligible?	no	yes	yes
Source of financial support	federal	institutional	institutional
Accepted at all colleges?	yes	depends	depends
Online or paper?	online	online	paper
Application fee	free	$25 plus $16 for every additional college	free

Grants

Grants are need-based financial assistance awarded based on a student's financial situation, such as family income, assets, and household size. The best part? They do not require repayment, making them essentially free money from the U.S. government, colleges, or private organizations. While federal grants are only available to U.S. citizens and permanent residents, international students may be eligible for grants awarded by colleges or other organizations.

> Grants are based on financial need and do not have to be repaid

Federal grant programs include the Teacher Education Assistance for College and Higher Education (TEACH) Grant, which provides up to $4,000 per year to students who commit to teaching at a low-income school after graduation. Based on their FAFSA, some students may also be awarded a Pell Grant[164], the federal grant for undergraduate students with financial need. The amount awarded through a Pell Grant is determined by the student's SAI, the cost of attendance, enrollment status (full-time or part-time), and plans to attend school for a full academic year. Pell Grant awards range from $700 to $7,000 per year, with the maximum amount adjusted annually by the U.S. Congress.

In addition to federal grants, many private foundations, such as the Bill and Melinda Gates Foundation, the Ford Foundation, and the Kellogg Foundation, also offer grant opportunities to college students. Grants used for non-educational purposes may be subject to taxation. Therefore, we recommend using grant money exclusively for educational expenses like tuition, fees, textbooks, and school supplies.

Find more info on federal grants at www.grants.gov

Scholarships

Grants are awarded based on a student's financial need, whereas scholarships are merit-based and granted for accomplishments in specific areas, such as academic excellence, athletic talent, artistic skill, leadership capabilities, or community engagement. Scholarships can be sponsored by colleges, private organizations, businesses, community groups, and individuals. They often cover educational expenses and occasionally include living expenses as well.

Scholarships are merit-based

Most scholarships have extensive application and selection processes. To receive a scholarship, recipients must meet specific eligibility requirements, such as maintaining a certain GPA or pursuing a particular field of study. Like grants, scholarships do not require repayment, making them an attractive way to (partially) finance your college education.

However, there is a potential caveat – some colleges limit the number of scholarships a student can utilize. Before applying to numerous scholarships, verify whether your college allows combining multiple scholarships. While stacking scholarships can significantly reduce your financial burden, many institutions have policies prohibiting this practice, known as scholarship displacement. This policy can lead to a reduction or even the removal of institutional scholarships provided by the college if you utilize multiple outside scholarships. In this case, you must choose the scholarship with the highest value or explore alternative financial aid options. To avoid complications, verify a college's scholarship policy on its website or contact its financial aid office and inquire about the threshold for external scholarships before they impact the institutional financial aid package.

> Verify if a college allows to stack scholarships

> National Merit Finalists & Scholars have admissions benefits and access to scholarships

The National Merit Scholarship Program is one of the most prominent scholarships recognizing American high school students for their academic achievements. The PSAT serves as the initial screening for the National Merit Scholarship Qualifying Test, which is why its official name is PSAT/NMSQT. Test takers who achieve top scores are designated National Merit Semi-Finalists.

In the next step, students submit detailed scholarship applications, including their academic records, extracurricular activities, leadership roles, an essay, and a letter of recommendation from a high school official[165]. From the Semi-Finalist pool, a select group is named National Merit Finalists. At the end of the selection process, about 2,500 students are awarded a scholarship as 'National Merit Scholar.' Receiving a National Merit Scholarship is highly regarded in the college admissions process, and a few colleges even award full-ride scholarships. Keep in mind that program participation is only available to citizens and green card holders attending high school inside or outside the United States.

Highly selective colleges prioritize need-based grants over merit-based scholarships; many, including the Ivy League colleges, are known for not offering merit aid at all. Instead, they offer generous need-based aid. This approach is not surprising because most – if not all – of their applicants are highly qualified. If you are ineligible for need-based aid but still require financial assistance, make sure to curate a well-rounded college list. Lower-tier colleges and safety schools often offer more merit aid than reach or target schools, as they consider you a top candidate.

> 'Ivy plus' schools offer generous need-based aid but typically no merit aid

Use these websites to find grants and scholarships:

- → https://bigfuture.collegeboard.org/pay-for-college
- → https://www.collegescholarships.org
- → https://www.ed.gov/
- → https://www.fastweb.com/
- → https://goodcall.com/
- → http://grants.gov
- → https://www.scholarships.com/
- → https://scholarships360.org/
- → https://studentaid.gov/understand-aid/types/grants
- → https://www.salliemae.com/scholarships/
- → https://www.unigo.com/

On-Campus Work

Working on campus is a common way to partially finance one's college education. Students typically have two options: participating in the Federal Work-Study Program or seeking regular part-time employment.

The federal Work-Study Program supports students with financial need

The Work-Study Program[166] is a federally funded program that provides part-time jobs for students with financial need. Jobs through this program may relate to the student's field of study or involve general administrative tasks, custodial work, or community service. To qualify for work-study, students must demonstrate financial need by completing the

Chapter 12 – Paying for College

FAFSA, which will determine the amount of work-study funding they receive. Work-study students are very attractive to employers, as the federal government subsidizes a portion of their wages. Students can use their earnings to help cover educational expenses such as tuition, fees, books, and living expenses. Payment is usually by the hour and must be at least the federal minimum wage. International students with an F-1 visa are not eligible for this program.

The second employment option is regular part-time on-campus work, which is available to all students regardless of their financial need. Students may work in various departments on campus, such as libraries, dining halls, administrative offices, or academic departments. Wages for regular on-campus jobs are determined by the college and are subject to minimum wage laws.

International students can work up to 20 hours per week during the academic year. However, they may work more during school breaks if they plan to enroll in the next academic term. They must obtain proper authorization from their Designated School Official before starting any on-campus job. All wages earned from on-campus employment are subject to taxation, and all students must comply with all relevant tax laws and regulations.

> F-1 students can work up to 20 hours per week on campus

Popular on-campus jobs include teaching assistants, research assistants, and resident advisors. These positions offer unique experiences and benefits. Teaching assistants, for instance, support professors by grading assignments, leading discussion sections, holding office hours, and sometimes delivering lectures. Research assistants work closely with faculty members on research projects, and their responsibilities often include literature reviews, data collection and analysis, experimental design, lab maintenance, or manuscript preparation. They may occasionally be able to co-author papers or present findings at conferences. TAs and RAs may be compensated by hourly wages or academic credit, so it is important to verify if and how much you get paid before taking on one of these roles.

> Verify whether TA and RA positions are for academic credit or paid jobs

Another popular position for on-campus work is to become a resident or community advisor. These advisors live in student housing and serve as peer mentors for the other students. Their responsibilities include organizing social programs (think pizza party or bingo night), enforcing community standards, and addressing concerns or conflicts. Resident advisors usually receive compensation in the form of free room and board, which significantly reduces the total cost of attendance.

> Resident advisors are compensated with free room and board

Student Loans

Student loans are funds that a student or their parents borrow to help pay for college expenses. Unlike scholarships and grants, they must be repaid with interest, the borrowing fee. Several types of student loans are available, including federal programs from the U.S.

> Loans need to be repaid with interest

government and loans from private banks. Repaying student loans usually begins after the student graduates, leaves school, or drops below half-time enrollment. Since the terms of the various loan options can vary significantly; it is important to fully understand the conditions and financial implications of each type of loan. Student loans can be obtained in three ways: directly by the student, their parents, or jointly.

Federal Loans Taken Out by the Student

As students have no or limited income, they cannot take out huge loans on their own. Still, the Federal Direct Loan Program allows students to borrow funds directly from the U.S. government. As the student signs and owns the loan, they are fully responsible for repaying it along with accrued interest. The federal program offers two types of loans directly to eligible students[167].

Direct subsidized loans are available to residents with demonstrated financial need. As a unique benefit, the government pays the loan interest while the student is in school. Direct subsidized loans are limited to $3,500 in the first year, $4,500 in the second, and $5,500 each in the third and following years, with a total subsidized loan limit of $23,000.

The second loan type offered by the Direct Loan Program includes direct unsubsidized loans, which are available to all residents regardless of financial needs. In this option, the government does not cover the interest while the student is enrolled in school, so interest starts accruing as soon as the loan is acquired.

A first-year student can borrow a maximum of $5,500

The combined annual loan limits for subsidized and unsubsidized federal loans are $5,500 in the first year, $6,500 in the second year, and $7,500 for the third year and beyond. The total limit of direct government loans is $31,000, meaning a student cannot take more federal loans during their entire undergraduate studies. Federal loans offer various repayment plans, including income-driven options that base monthly payments on the borrower's income. International students are not eligible for federal loans.

Federal Loans Taken Out by the Parents

Since first-year students can only borrow a maximum of $5,500 on their own, they may need their parents' support to secure additional loans beyond the direct federal loan limits. One option to obtain additional funds is the Parent PLUS loan[168]. The U.S. government offers these loans to eligible parents of dependent undergraduate students. They are signed and owned by the parents, not the student, hence the name. The maximum loan amount is the cost of attendance minus any other financial aid the student has received. These loans require a credit check and have higher interest rates than direct student loans.

> Parents, not the student, own the Parent PLUS loan

Private Loans Taken Out Jointly

In addition to federal loans, private banks, credit unions, and online lenders offer private student loans. Students usually lack the credit score and income to qualify for a private loan, so they require a parent or other family member as a co-signer.

In this setup, the student and family member share ownership of the loan contract and are equally responsible for repaying it with accrued interest. If the student fails to make payments, the parent, as a co-signer, is legally obligated to repay the entire loan amount and any accrued interest and fees. Late or missed payments on the loan can negatively impact both the student's and the parents' credit scores, making it more challenging to qualify for future loans or credit cards. If a co-signer dies, the lender may require the loan to be repaid in full immediately – which will likely be a challenge for the student. In addition, private loans usually have significantly higher interest rates than federal ones.

Given these potential risks, the student and their family should carefully consider the implications of co-signing a loan and explore alternative options for financing their college. If eligible, it is advisable to opt for federal student loans, as they offer more favorable terms, such as fixed lower interest rates, income-driven repayment plans, and forgiveness options that private loans may not have.

> Co-signers are equally responsible for repaying a private loan

The table on the next page summarizes the terms of federal and private student loans for the 2024/25 academic year.

Overview of typical student loans in 2024/25[4]:

		Direct Federal Subsidized Loan	Direct Federal Unsubsidized Loan	Federal Parent PLUS Loan	Private Loans
Loan limit	1st year	$3,500	$5,500 (with a maximum of $3,500 subsidized)	Cost of attendance minus any financial assistance	depends
	2nd year	$4,500	$6,500 (with a maximum of $4,500 subsidized)		
	3rd year & beyond	$5,500	$7,500 (with a maximum of $5,500 subsidized)		
Interest rates (2024/25)		6.53%	6.53%	9.08%	up to 15%
Interest accrued?		no	yes	yes	yes
International students?		no	no	no	yes

Illustration of the Financial Implications of Various Loan Types[169]

To examine the financial implications of various loan types, let us consider a case where a first-year student, Lauren, borrows a specific amount every year for four years. The table below compares four

---

[4] Always verify current terms and conditions. All numbers and calculations are based on the Student Loan Projector Calculator at: calculator.net.

Chapter 12 – Paying for College

scenarios: a direct subsidized student loan, a direct unsubsidized student loan, a Parent PLUS loan, and a private co-signed loan.

	Scenario 1 Direct Subsidized	Scenario 2 Direct Unsubsidized	Scenario 3 Parent PLUS	Scenario 4 Private Lender
Loan Type	student loan, subsidized	student loan, unsubsidized	parent loan, unsubsidized	co-signed loan, unsubsidized
Interest accrued?	no	yes	yes	yes
Graduates after	4 years			
Co-signer?	no	no	yes	yes
Annual loan	$3,500	$3,500	$20,000	$20,000
Interest rate	6.53%	6.53%	9.08%	14%
Total loan	$14,000	$14,000	$80,000	$80,000
Balance after 4 years	$14,000	$15,949	$96,026	$106,430
Loan term	10 years			
Monthly repayments	$159	$181	$1,221	$1,652
Total interest over 10 years	$5,102	$7,761	$66,470	$118,300
Total payments over 10 years	$19,102	$23,710	$146,470	$198,300

In a realistic scenario, Lauren may take two loans: a direct loan and an additional one with her parents to cover her cost of attendance. After four years, Lauren has taken out a total loan of $14,000 (scenarios 1 and 2) or $80,000 (scenarios 3 and 4) through her parents. Upon graduation, she begins making monthly payments. When she finally has repaid her student loan including interest after ten years, she has paid significantly more interest for the private loan ($118,300) than the principal amount ($80,000) she borrowed.

The table highlights how interest rates substantially impact the total payments over the loan's 10-year lifespan. Federal loans have lower interest rates than private ones, and those taken out directly by the students have the most favorable terms. In our example, taking a federal Parent PLUS loan with an interest rate of 9.08% will result in lower monthly payments and $50,000 less interest paid than a private loan at a 14% interest rate. This example demonstrates the clear advantage of prioritizing federal loans over private ones due to their lower interest rates and overall cost.

> Interest rates are the biggest factor in student loans

A commonly cited rule of thumb is not to borrow more than your expected starting salary after graduation. This means that your total student loan debt should be less than what you expect to earn in your first year of work. Based on this rule, Lauren should secure a starting salary of at least $14,000 in

> Don't borrow more than your starting salary after graduation

Chapter 12 – Paying for College

scenario 1 to comfortably repay her loan – a reasonable expectation for most jobs requiring a college degree.

However, in scenario 4, she would need a starting salary of at least $106,430 (the outstanding balance after graduation) to manage her student loan repayments. Not all majors have six-digit starting salaries, putting students at risk of struggling to repay their loans. Exercising prudence and adhering to reasonable borrowing limits that are aligned with one's expected post-graduation income is crucial to avoid excessive debt.

> International students are not eligible for federal student loans

Keep in mind that international students are not eligible for federal student loans. If unable to pay for their college education out-of-pocket, they must consider private loans from a bank in their home country or find an American lender willing to work with international students. Interest rates and fees on international student loans are often higher than those obtained with a U.S. co-signer. Some colleges offer institutional loans to international students to help cover educational expenses.

To summarize, while student loans can provide access to higher education, they can also significantly impact your future financials and the ability to secure other types of loans in the future. If possible, avoid taking out any college loans, and if you must take one, carefully consider its terms and conditions!

> Avoid taking out student loans unless absolutely necessary

Negotiating Your Financial Aid Award

What if you find that your financial aid is not enough to cover all expenses? It may surprise you, but you can negotiate financial terms with colleges. This process, known as appealing for more financial aid, involves formally requesting the college to reconsider your aid package based on additional information you provide. This could be a change in your financial circumstances or new information not included in your original application.

The appeal process varies, but generally, you must submit a written appeal via email or traditional mail. For a successful appeal, you cannot just ask for more money but must present a strong case. If a new financial hardship was not captured in your original application,

> Appeal for more need-based aid if your financial situation has changed

you might be successful with your appeal for more need-based aid. This could include events like divorce, the addition of a new family member, the death of a parent, a recent illness or disability, increased childcare expenses, or any other unforeseen financial occurrence. Reach out to the office of financial assistance to ask for more need-based aid.

> Appeal for more merit aid if you have become a more competitive candidate

Provide new, factual reasons to increase your chances of successfully appealing for more merit aid. Colleges are more likely to negotiate if you are a competitive applicant. Compelling evidence could include a significantly improved GPA or a new major award. Some schools may adjust their award package to match a better financial offer from another college. In this case, emphasize in your letter that the institution you are appealing to is your preferred choice but stress that the other school is a more affordable option. Include a copy of their financial aid letter as supporting evidence. Contact the admissions office directly to ask for more merit aid.

Only commit to a college once you have received all financial aid offers. Take your time to evaluate all offers and find the college that best fits your academic, personal, and financial situation. File your appeal as soon as you know of your financial needs, but preferably before the May 1 commitment deadline. However, if your circumstances change later, you can still submit an appeal, even after committing to it – your college may still consider your request. When appealing for more aid, avoid using the term 'negotiation' and, instead, use 'reconsideration.' Do not be afraid to ask for more money, as colleges will not rescind offers based on an appeal, but be realistic in your request.

File your appeal before May 1

Making a Rational Decision

Given the rising cost of attending an American college, let us look at some effective strategies for finding affordable options, guided by rational factors rather than emotions.

While many applicants have a 'dream school' based on prestige or reputation, it is wiser to consider colleges with a good academic, social, and financial fit. Remember, it is not about a brand name but about finding a place where you can thrive academically, socially, and financially. Use the Net Price Calculator to estimate your total cost and consider colleges you can afford to attend. Think like an investor and calculate the potential return on investment of your education by comparing the cost of attendance to your expected starting salary and potential earnings after five years in the workforce.

> Find a college where you can thrive academically, socially, & financially

Avoid going into debt for your college education. If you must borrow money, start with federal loans, particularly subsidized ones, as they offer more favorable terms and repayment options than private loans. Be mindful of the long-term consequences of taking on debt and borrow only what you need to cover educational expenses.

To reduce the overall expenses for your undergraduate degree, consider starting at a community college and then transferring to a four-year institution. In addition, apply strategically and cast a wide net that includes additional safety schools that may offer merit-based aid. Academic scholarships are awarded based on your achievements rather than financial need and can significantly reduce your college expenses. As a strong contender for your safety schools, you may be eligible for generous scholarships.

Chapter 12 – Paying for College

If you intend to pursue a graduate degree, keep your undergraduate expenses in check. Do not spend all your college funds on attending an expensive undergraduate program if you know you will continue on to graduate school. Post-graduation, the name of your undergraduate alma mater becomes less influential. Instead, employers are more likely to prioritize your advanced degree, the knowledge acquired during graduate school, and your work ethic. By planning ahead, you can minimize your overall financial commitment.

> Save funds for graduate school

Start saving for college as early as possible or consider taking a gap year to work and save money before enrolling. A gap year is a year-long break between high school and college where you can work, travel, or volunteer. This can be a great opportunity to gain real-world experience, save money, and clarify your academic and career goals before enrolling in college. Explore part-time job opportunities while in college to earn extra income. In addition, actively seek out scholarships and grants to supplement your financial aid package and reduce your overall college expenses.

Chapter 13 – The Visa Process

Except for an English proficiency test for non-native speakers, the college application process for international students mirrors that of U.S. residents. Yet, once admitted, a college must sponsor a visa to allow an international student to enter and reside in the United States lawfully. This chapter provides an overview of the application process and offers strategies to improve your chances of having your F-1 student visa approved.

Overview of the Visa Process

Before we dive into the specifics of the visa process, let us reiterate a crucial aspect – it is worth repeating. Ensure, before you apply, that your prospective college is approved for the Student and Exchange Visitor Program, as only participating colleges can sponsor student visas. The U.S. Homeland Security's website provides a comprehensive list of all approved institutions[170]. You do not want to find yourself in a situation where a college admits you but cannot sponsor you for a student visa!

> Verify that a college can sponsor a student visa *before* applying

Chapter 13 – The Visa Process

Once you have accepted the admissions offer, the school's international office will register you in the Student and Exchange Visitor Information System and issue Form I-20. After paying the SEVIS I-901 fee of $350, you can apply for an F-1 visa at a U.S. embassy in your home country by completing Form DS-160 online and attending an in-person interview. New student visas can be issued up to 365 days in advance, but students can only enter the U.S. up to 30 days before their program begins. Given the variation in wait times for interview appointments and visa processing times, applying at least three months before your term begins is recommended.

SEVIS I-901 fee: $350

As part of the DS-160 application, you provide personal and educational data and pay a non-refundable fee. You must also include Form I-20, which you and the school official must have signed beforehand. During the interview, a consular officer will evaluate your eligibility based on your application, academic records, commitment to depart after your studies, and ability to cover all expenses. They will also take digital fingerprint scans.

DS-160 fee: $185

If approved, the embassy will mail your passport containing the F-1 visa or instruct you to collect it in person. Keep in mind that a visa does not guarantee entry into the United States; it merely allows the holder to travel to an American port of entry, such as an airport, and request permission to enter. Homeland Security and Customs and Border Protection officials have the ultimate authority to permit or deny entry.

MISSION: ACCEPTED!

Overview of the steps to obtain an F-1 student visa:

	SEVP-approved college	International applicant
Enroll applicants at the college	✓	✓
Register student for SEVIS	✓	
Issue Form I-20	✓	
Pay SEVIS I-901 ($350)		✓
Complete online application		✓
Pay DS-160 fee ($185)		✓
Schedule & attend interview		✓

Documents required for the F-1 visa application:

- ☐ I-20 certificate
- ☐ Receipt of your SEVIS I-901 fee
- ☐ Receipt of the online DS-160 visa form and payment
- ☐ Passport valid six months beyond your intended stay
- ☐ Any old passports
- ☐ Documents that prove your financial funds
- ☐ Two recent color photos
- ☐ Transcripts, test scores, and qualifications from prior schools
- ☐ Proof of your ties to your home country and intent to return

As the primary applicant, you will be granted an F-1 student visa. You can apply for dependent visas if you plan to bring your spouse or children. If approved, your spouse and minor children are eligible for an F-2 dependent visa, allowing them to accompany you. You and your dependents must depart the United States within 60 days after the program end date listed on your Form I-20. Always check the homepage of the U.S. Department of Homeland Security[171] for the most recent updates.

Required Forms

Now that we understand the process to apply for a student visa, let us examine the various forms needed.

Form I-20

Your college will provide you with the Form I-20, the 'Certificate of Eligibility for Nonimmigrant (F-1) Student Status – For Academic and Language Students'. This form certifies your admission to a U.S. college and your eligibility to apply for the F-1 student visa. You will present the I-20 during your interview and again when entering the United States. The form contains detailed information regarding the sponsoring college, your field of study, and the parameters for permissible work, such as on-campus jobs and required or optional practical training. In addition, the form outlines the estimated annual cost of attendance and how you plan to pay for them. You must have this amount reflected in your bank statement before your interview.

Typical costs and funding sources specified in Form I-20

Estimated costs		Estimated student funding	
Tuition and fees:	$...	Personal funds	$...
Living expenses	$...	Scholarships	$...
Expenses of dependents	$...	Family funds	$...
Other	$...	On-campus employment	$...

Form SEVIS I-901

SEVIS, the Student and Exchange Visitor Information System, is an online platform that maintains records of all non-immigrant students. Once your college registers you in the SEVIS system, you will use Form SEVIS I-901 to pay the $350 fee. To settle this fee, visit *fmjfee.com*. Print the receipt, which you must present at your visa interview.

Form DS-160

After obtaining your I-20 form, being registered in the SEVIS system, and paying the I-901 fee, you can apply for a non-immigrant visa through the Department of State's[172] website at *https://ceac.state.gov/genniv/*. To apply for the visa, you fill out Form DS-160, which collects personal information, travel plans, and details about your qualifications for the student visa. Write down the Application ID displayed in the website's top right-hand corner, as you need it to access your application later. The system will automatically time out after 20 minutes of inactivity, so make sure to save your application frequently

Chapter 13 – The Visa Process

to avoid losing any information. All answers must be in English except for your name, which may be written in your native alphabet. Translations of the questions are available in many languages on the website. You must answer all mandatory questions; if a question does not apply to your situation, write 'does not apply.'

Required documents for Form DS-160:

- ☐ Passport
- ☐ Travel itinerary (if you have already made arrangements)
- ☐ Dates of your last five visits to the United States
- ☐ International travel history for the past five years
- ☐ Curriculum Vitae: previous education and work history
- ☐ Your SEVIS ID (printed on your I-20)
- ☐ Address of the college (printed on your I-20)

After completing the form, print and retain the DS-160 barcode and confirmation number, as you must present them at your visa interview. It is not necessary to print the entire application. You are responsible for scheduling a visa interview; the embassy will not schedule the appointment for you! Refer to the website of the U.S. embassy responsible for your home country for specific guidelines. Verify the visa wait times and schedule your interview as early as possible. Next, you must pay the visa application processing fee of $185. Check the embassy or consulate's website for country-specific payment instructions. Keep the payment receipt, as you must present it during your interview.

Preparing for Your Visa Interview

The in-person interview at the U.S. embassy is the final step in obtaining your student visa. This appointment determines whether your visa application is granted, making thorough preparation crucial. During the interview, the consular officer wants to learn more about you beyond what your documents present. They seek to confirm your genuine intention to study in the United States and verify that you have no ulterior motives.

The interviewer verifies your motivations, ability to pay, and intention to leave the U.S. after graduation

Make sure you have all the necessary documents, including admission letters, academic records, and financial statements. Be prepared to discuss your chosen program and how it aligns with your career goals in your home country. Demonstrating thorough knowledge about faculty, research opportunities, and program specifics can positively impact your interview. Contact your college's Designated School Official for school-specific advice to help you prepare for your interview.

Financial documents:
-Bank statements
-Sponsor letter
-Financial aid letter
-Scholarship letter
-Employment & salary

In addition, you must also prove you have sufficient financial means to cover all costs associated with your first year of studies. Typically, this involves providing certification from a financial institution confirming the availability of funds. Do not rely on potential employment in the U.S. to cover

Chapter 13 – The Visa Process

expenses, as this may lead to visa denial. While scholarships can help, they usually do not cover all costs, so ensure you have additional funding sources like personal savings or family support. Bring original copies of all required documents and certified translations if your documents are in a language other than English.

List of documents to bring to the interview:

- ☐ Form DS-160 confirmation page, including the barcode
- ☐ Form I-20
- ☐ SEVIS I-901 fee receipt (payment must be made at *www.fmjfee.com* at least three days before your interview)
- ☐ One 5 x 5 cm (2" by 2") color photograph taken within the last six months using U.S. photo requirements
- ☐ Your passport containing at least one blank page. For certain nationalities, the passport must be valid for at least six months beyond the proposed stay in the U.S.
- ☐ Previously issued U.S. visa(s), if applicable
- ☐ Evidence of financial ability (bank statements showing sufficient funds, sponsorship letters, scholarships, etc.)
- ☐ Admission letter(s)
- ☐ Academic records (transcripts, IB diplomas, certificates, etc.)
- ☐ Standardized test scores (SAT, ACT, TOEFL, IELTS, Duolingo)
- ☐ Evidence of your intent to return to your home country
- ☐ Documentation of any arrests, convictions, or cautions, even if they are regarded as spent.
- ☐ If you have previously faced entry denial, deportation, or removal from the U.S., you may need additional documents.

Be prepared to convincingly demonstrate your strong ties to your home country and your intention to return after completing your studies. This may involve discussing your close family relationships, future career opportunities, financial assets, or property holdings in your home country. Emphasizing these ties helps reduce any potential suspicions that you might be planning to illegally immigrate into the U.S. Practice speaking about your goals, background, and plans before your appointment in a mock interview with a friend, teacher, or family member. Prepare specific and convincing responses to common interview questions.

> Bring certified translations of all non-English documents

Possible interview questions and answer strategies:

→ *Why do you want to study in the U.S.?*
  Highlight how specific aspects of the U.S. education system align with your academic and career goals, and emphasize how a U.S. education will help your career in your home country.

→ *How many colleges did you apply to, how many accepted you, and how many did not?*
  The question aims to understand your academic and professional potential. Admission to more prestigious universities may enhance your visa prospects. Be truthful about your rejections, as dishonesty may jeopardize your visa application.

- → *What will you specialize in?*
  Be specific about your field of study and how it relates to your future career path.

- → *Why did you choose this university?*
  Discuss the university's reputation, the faculty's expertise, and how the program fits your interests.

- → *How do you plan to fund your studies?*
  Detail your financial plan, mentioning scholarships, family support, or savings. Explain how your family members or other sponsors can afford to support you financially.

- → *Can you prove your financial stability?*
  Be ready to present bank statements, scholarship letters, or sponsorship letters.

- → *What are your plans after completing your studies?*
  Emphasize your intent to return to your home country and apply the knowledge gained in your field. Be specific when outlining your career plans in your home country.

- → *Do you know any professors at the university? What are their names and their research interests?*
  Showing knowledge about the faculty demonstrates genuine interest in the academic environment.

- → *What specific courses are you looking forward to?*
  Mention courses and how they are relevant to your career goals.

- → *Have you been to the United States before?*
  Your travel history can show previous compliance with U.S. laws.

- → *Do you have family or friends in the U.S.?*
  Acknowledge your family connections in the U.S., but emphasize your stronger ties and commitments to your home country.

→ *What are your plans after graduation?*
Explain how your U.S. degree will help your professional life in your home country.

→ *Why do you deserve a student visa?*
This question is your opportunity to present a compelling argument for why you merit the visa. Remember to mention that you will return to your home country after graduating.

Dress appropriately for the interview, arrive early, and answer questions to the point without unnecessary elaboration. If you rely on someone else sponsoring your expenses, choose a close relative rather than a distant cousin or family friend. Provide truthful answers – inconsistencies or incorrect facts can lead to visa denial.

Common reasons for visa rejection include lack of financial proof and insufficient evidence of intent to return to your home country after completing your studies. Other potential reasons are incomplete or incorrect documentation, an unsuccessful background check, or the inability to articulate your responses clearly.

If your visa application is denied, you can reapply up to three times within twelve months. To reapply, you must reinitiate the DS-160 application process and pay the application fees again, although the SEVIS fee is waived for applications within the same year. Upon denial, you will receive an explanation for the decision; be sure to address these issues to improve your chances of approval in future attempts. However, if you

> You may reapply up to three times

Maintaining Your F-1 Status

The U.S. Department of State issues your visa with the understanding that your main reason for visiting is your college education. To maintain your visa status, you must adhere to your educational goals and follow all visa regulations. International students must enter the country no more than 30 days before the start of their program. Upon arrival, international students must meet with their Designated School Official before the program start date specified in Form I-20.

Maintain a full academic course load

To maintain your F-1 student status, you must enroll in a full course of study each term and progress academically. Your DSO is your primary contact for any questions about your stay, including changes to your major, taking a break, international travel, moving, or requesting extensions. Consult your DSO before dropping any classes or if you need a program extension, which must be requested before your I-20 program end date. To qualify for annual vacation, students must complete a full academic year and intend to enroll for the upcoming term. F-1 students can work under specific conditions, but unauthorized employment will have severe consequences. Upon completing your studies, you have a 60-day grace period to leave the United States, transfer to another college, change education levels, or adjust your visa status.

Do not work without permission

Families with a Non-Immigrant Visa

Some families reside in the United States under a temporary, non-immigrant visa, such as the L1 visa for intracompany transfers, E2 visa for business investors, or H-1B visa for specialty occupations. For these families, it is critical to understand the implications of their visa status for their children's college education. Even if their children have graduated from a U.S. high school, they are typically classified as international students since they are neither citizens nor permanent residents.

> Dependent children must obtain their own visa when they marry or turn 21

Generally, as long as the parents' visa status remains valid and they fulfill the visa requirements, their dependent children can stay in the U.S. under the same visa category. However, if the parents' visa status changes or expires, their dependent children must obtain their own visa or leave the United States. In addition, children of non-immigrant visa holders can only remain on their parents' visa if unmarried and under 21 years old.

Therefore, admitted students should apply for an F-1 student visa as soon as they receive acceptance from a college. This ensures they can maintain their legal status throughout their college education, independently from any changes or restrictions of their parents' visa status. Not doing so could lead to potential complications and even the need to leave the country.

Checklists

(* specific to international students)

International Students: Before You Apply

- ☐ Verify that a potential college is approved for visa sponsoring in the Student and Exchange Visitor Program
- ☐ Check that your English proficiency results (TOEFL or IELTS) pass the expected minimum score for all potential colleges
- ☐ Transcript with predicted grades for senior year (if needed)
- ☐ Certified translation of your transcript
- ☐ Third-party evaluation of your transcripts (if needed)
- ☐ Passport
- ☐ Verify that you have all required immunizations
- ☐ Get your financial documentation certifying that you can afford the first year of college

Documents Needed for the Visa Interview

- ☐ Certificate of Eligibility for non-immigrant students (I-20)
- ☐ Receipt of SEVIS I-901 fee
- ☐ Receipt of DS-160 visa form
- ☐ Passport valid at least six months beyond your intended period of stay
- ☐ Any old passports

- [ ] Documents that prove your financial funds: Family bank statements, documentation from a sponsor, financial aid and scholarship letters, employment letter showing annual salary
- [ ] Two recent color photos
- [ ] Transcripts, test scores, qualifications, or certificates from all prior schools
- [ ] Documents proving ties to your home country and intent to return

Year-by-Year To-Do List for Grades 9 through 12

(* specific to international students)

Freshman year (Grade 9)

- [ ] Give yourself time to adjust to high school
- [ ] Map out your potential classes for grades 10 through 12
- [ ] Begin researching your career interests
- [ ] Fix any academic issues, especially in math and English
- [ ] Explore options for a potential passion project, internships, or leadership opportunities

Sophomore year (Grade 10)

- [ ] Get the best grades you can
- [ ] Study for the PSAT
- [ ] Choose your AP, IB and other diploma classes wisely
- [ ] Fix any academic issues, especially in math and English
- [ ] Explore options for a potential passion project, internships, or leadership opportunities

Checklists

Summer before Junior Year (Grade 10 to 11)

- ☐ Set up an email address that sounds professional
- ☐ Create accounts for the Common App, UC App, CSU App, or other apps used by prospective colleges to familiarize yourself with their requirements
- ☐ Create a balanced list of safety, target, and reach schools
- ☐ Maintain a spreadsheet to keep track of all college details
- ☐ Visit each college's website. Take note of the following for each school:
  - o Regular and early application deadlines
  - o Application requirements
  - o Standardized testing strategy: SAT/ACT required, test-flexible, test-optional, test-blind?
  - o Supplemental essays or questions
  - o Specific programs of interest
- ☐ Plan and attend in-person or virtual campus tours, admissions events, etc.
- ☐ Schedule and begin studying for any tests that you are planning to take: PSAT, SAT, ACT, AP, English proficiency tests (TOEFL or IELTS)*
- ☐ Fill any academic gaps that you may have (review yourself, online or in-person tutoring)
- ☐ Explore your career interests
- ☐ Tour college campuses online or in-person
- ☐ Do something meaningful to you (travel, internship, summer job, explore a new hobby)!

Junior Year (Grade 11)

- ☐ Get the best grades you can
- ☐ Schedule and take the PSAT as practice and baseline for the SAT
- ☐ Register for and take the SAT or ACT (do this early enough to allow time for retaking)
- ☐ Register for any AP or IB exams
- ☐ Study for and take the language proficiency test*
- ☐ Research options to get your transcripts translated and, if needed, evaluated*
- ☐ Plan your letters of recommendation
    - o Write a brag sheet
    - o Ask two subject teachers for recommendations
    - o Ask someone outside of school for a letter of recommendation
    - o Send your brag sheet to all recommenders and your school counselor
- ☐ Continue to research the colleges on your balanced list and reduce it to a manageable number
- ☐ Continue to tour college campuses online or in-person

Summer before Senior Year (Grade 11 to 12)

- ☐ Beginning August 1, verify the current essay prompts in the Common App and begin drafting and revising your essays
- ☐ Have your transcripts translated or evaluated*
- ☐ Continue with your passion project and other activities
- ☐ Begin writing your activity list
- ☐ Tour campuses (in-person or virtual)
- ☐ Study for any test you are planning to take or retake in the fall
- ☐ Have some fun!

Checklists

Beginning of Senior Year (Grade 12)

- ☐ Revise and proofread your essays and incorporate feedback
- ☐ Revise and enter your activity list
- ☐ Send standardized test scores with your application
- ☐ Self-report your courses and grades in the application
- ☐ Have your TOEFL / IELTS results sent to colleges*
- ☐ Have your translated/evaluated transcripts sent to colleges*
- ☐ Send invite link (or instructions) to teachers and counselor writing your letters of recommendation
- ☐ Finalize, proofread, and submit your **early applications** at least one or two days before the deadline. Websites may crash on the day of the deadline. Note: All deadlines are the college's local time, not your local time zone!
- ☐ When prompted, set up your college-specific portal

Fall through Winter of Senior Year (Grade 12)

- ☐ Finalize, proofread, and submit your **regular decision applications** at least one or two days before the deadline. Websites may crash on the day of the deadline. Remember: All deadlines are the college's local time, not your local time zone.
- ☐ Tell your school counselor that you applied or update Naviance or SCOIR
- ☐ When prompted, set up your college-specific portal
- ☐ Monitor your email and all portals for any communication from the colleges
- ☐ Send additional material if needed
- ☐ Interview with admissions officer or alumni
- ☐ Request that the high school transcript and quarter/ midyear grade report be sent to colleges
- ☐ Submit FAFSA if eligible
- ☐ Submit CSS Profile or ISFAA if needed

- ☐ Keep your grades up
- ☐ Send thank-you notes to recommenders and school counselor
- ☐ Research and apply for scholarships
- ☐ Don't go crazy waiting for results!

Before May 1 (Senior Spring)

- ☐ Receive decision letters
- ☐ If waitlisted, send a letter of continued interest and any requested updates
- ☐ Attend admitted student days
- ☐ Decide which college to attend
- ☐ Commit to your college in their portal by May 1
- ☐ Withdraw applications to other colleges you will not attend
- ☐ Apply for scholarships
- ☐ Apply for F-1 student visa*
- ☐ Schedule an appointment in the U.S. embassy *
- ☐ Maintain your senior grades

May 1 until Summer after Senior Year

- ☐ Take senior year AP or IB exams
- ☐ Take national graduation exams: Abitur, A-levels, Bac*
- ☐ Have your high school send your final (evaluated/translated*) transcript
- ☐ Apply for housing and meal plans
- ☐ Apply for F-1 student visa at U.S. embassy or consulate*
- ☐ Accept financial aid offer
- ☐ Enroll in or waive health insurance
- ☐ Verify immunization requirements
- ☐ Plan your move
- ☐ Remember: College is what you make of it!

Further Reading

Bruni, F. (2023). *Where You Go is Not Who You'll Be: An Antidote to the College Admissions Mania. Updated edition.* Grand Central Publishing.

Corcoran, M. (2021). *Year by Year to College. For IB and International Students.* College Success Press

Duolingo English Test. www.englishtest.duolingo.com

Fiske, E. (2024). *Fiske Guide to Colleges 2025. 41st Edition.* Sourcebooks (release date: 07/09/2024)

IELTS International. www.ielts.org. E-mail: stakeholders@ieltsusa.org

Sawyer, E. (2016). *College Essay Essentials. A Step-by-Step Guide to Writing a Successful College Admissions Essay.* Sourcebooks

Sawyer, E. (2020). *College Admissions Essentials. A Step-by-Step Guide to Showing Colleges Who You Are and What Matters to You.* Sourcebooks

Selingo, J. (2020). *Who Gets in and Why. A Year inside College Admissions.* Scribner.

Student loan calculator: https://www.calculator.net/student-loan-calculator.html

Tanabe, G. & Tanabe, K. (2019). *50 Successful University of California Application Essays. Get into the Top UC colleges and Other Selective Schools. Third Edition.* SuperCollege

Tanabe, G. & Tanabe, K. (2018). *50 Successful Stanford Application Essays. Write Your Way into the College of Your Choice. Third Edition.* SuperCollege

TOEFL Services. www.toefl.org. E-mail: toefl@ets.org

U.S. Department of Homeland Security. *Study in the States.* https://studyinthestates.dhs.gov/

Walker, B.V. (2017). *Never Pay Retail for College. How Smart Parents Find the Right School for the Right Price.* Prussian Press

Wissner-Gross, E. (2006). *What Colleges Don't Tell you (and Other Parents Don't Want You to Know). 272 Secrets for Getting Your Kid into the Top Schools.* Penguin Group

Yale News (2020). *50 Yale Admission Success Stories & the Essays that Made Them Happen.* St. Martin's Griffin

About the Author

Christine Hees is an experienced marketing professional and passionate advocate for education. After graduating with a Bachelor's degree in Business and Computer Science, she worked at a leading computer corporation. During her tenure, she held various leadership positions in global and European marketing functions. Christine lived and worked in Germany, Austria, and France before relocating to Mountain View, California, where she resides with her husband and three children. To combat the COVID-19 lockdown blues, Christine enrolled at Foothill College, where she earned an AA in Psychology. Her journey into understanding the American college admissions process began while supporting her two oldest children through their applications. Struck by the differences from her own experience, Christine became determined to demystify the process. She firmly believes that a profound knowledge of college admissions can contribute to making higher education more accessible.

References

[1] NCES (2023). *Public School Enrollment.* https://nces.ed.gov/programs/coe/indicator/cga/public-school-enrollment

[2] Morse, R. & Brooks, E. (2023). *How States Compare in the 2023-2024 Best High Schools Rankings.* US News and World Report. https://www.usnews.com/education/best-high-schools/articles/how-states-compare#:~:text=Massachusetts%20tops%20all%20other%20states,top%2Dranked%20public%20high%20schools.&text=%7C-,Aug.,2023%2C%20at%209%3A00%20p.m.&text=A%20breakdown%20by%20state%20of,once%20again%20the%20leading%20performer

[3] Niche (2024). *2024 Best School Districts in America.* https://www.niche.com/k12/search/best-school-districts/

[4] California Department of Education (2024). *State Minimum High School Graduation Requirements.* https://www.cde.ca.gov/ci/gs/hs/hsgrmin.asp

[5] College Board (2024). *How long does my AP score remain valid?.* https://international.collegeboard.org/help-center/how-long-does-my-ap-score-remain-valid

[6] College Board (2024). *Can I sign up to retake an AP Exam?.* https://apstudents.collegeboard.org/help-center/can-i-sign-retake-ap-exam#:~:text=AP%20Exams%20are%20only%20given,one%20be%20withheld%20or%20canceled.

[7] International Baccalaureate Organization (2023). *Facts and Figures.* https://www.ibo.org/about-the-ib/facts-and-figures/

[8] Crimson Education (2023). *IB Students Acceptance Rates at the Top 25 US Universities.* https://pages.crimsoneducation.org/rs/039-NBM-750/images/FL-10-2018-ib-student-acceptance-rates-at-top-us-

universities.pdf?mkt_tok=eyJpIjoiWTJaalltRTJOV0kzT1#:~:text=There%20are%20many%20other%20factors,top%20of%20the%20admissions%20pool

[9] International Baccalaureate Organization (2023). *Diploma Program.* https://www.ibo.org/programmes/diploma-programme/

[10] GPA Calculator (2024). https://gpacalculator.net/high-school-gpa-calculator/

[11] University of California (2023). *IB Credits.* https://admission.universityofcalifornia.edu/admission-requirements/ap-exam-credits/ib-credits.html

[12] Boston University (2023). *International Baccalaureate Guide. Course Equivalence 2023-2024.* https://www.bu.edu/admissions/files/2018/05/ib_course_equivalence.pdf

[13] College Board (2023). *SAT Suite of Assessment.* https://satsuite.collegeboard.org/sat

[14] College Board (2024). *Download Bluebook.* https://bluebook.collegeboard.org/students/download-bluebook

[15] ACT (2024). https://www.act.org/content/act/en/register-for-the-act.html?utm_medium=paidsearch&utm_source=google&utm_campaign=fy24q2-fy24q3-spring+summer-national---paid-digital-k12-b2c&utm_content=dc_1720-internal-paid-040824-mr032606-&utm_term=act&utm_campaign=Google%7CSearch%7CIntent%7CB2C%7CCPC%7CJune+ACT+2023%7C4/3/2023-5/19/2023%7CDesktop&utm_source=adwords&utm_medium=ppc&hsa_acc=5799955628&hsa_cam=21152139297&hsa_grp=160651264077&hsa_ad=695727513305&hsa_src=g&hsa_tgt=aud-1679357477266:kwd-12546200&hsa_kw=act&hsa_mt=e&hsa_net=adwords&hsa_ver=3&gad_source=1&gclid=Cj0KCQjw6PGxBhCVARIsAIumnWYQxQznVQUm-u05PX9cQ_4DoaOU_kjovnS5ql-lWppvNvn5NJEdAn8aAtDBEALw_wcB

[16] MIT (2023). *Tests & scores.* https://mitadmissions.org/apply/firstyear/tests-scores/

[17] Berger, R. (2022). *Democratizing The College Admissions Process Is Big Business.* Forbes. https://www.forbes.com/sites/rodberger/2022/05/23/democratizing-the-college-admissions-process-is-big-business/?sh=4ef57f2569c9

[18] Kaplan Test Prep (2023). https://www.kaptest.com/

[19] The Princeton Review (2024). *Maximum Results. Minimum Time.* https://www.princetonreview.com/?ExDT=2&gad_source=1&gclid=Cj0KCQiA

References

homtBhDgARIsABcaYylEG1gm2-LLDjfTDjCwcDDaFPsOmhfbdewspssukPQqlwYeAnF5-ikaAivXEALw_wcB

[20] Khan Academy (2023). *Maximize your score with free Official Digital SAT Prep.* https://www.khanacademy.org/digital-sat

[21] Galegos, E. & Willis, D.J. (2024). *Most California high school seniors shut out of even applying to the state's universities.* https://www.sfchronicle.com/california/article/california-high-school-seniors-can-t-apply-18665664.php

[22] Texas A&M University (2024). *University Facts.* https://www.tamu.edu/about/facts.html

[23] California Community Colleges (2024). *Transfer.* https://www.cccco.edu/Students/Transfer

[24] Harvard University (2024). *Supporting Our Mission.* https://www.harvard.edu/about/endowment/

[25] National Center for Educational Statistics (2023). *Characteristics of Degree-Granting Postsecondary Institutions.* https://nces.ed.gov/programs/coe/indicator/csa/postsecondary-institutions#:~:text=In%20academic%20year%202021%E2%80%9322%2C%20there%20were%203%2C542%20degree%2D,1%20with%20first%2Dyear%20undergraduates

[26] Ivy Scholars (2024). *Have Ivy League Acceptance Rates Changed?.* https://www.ivyscholars.com/2021/09/07/have-ivy-league-acceptance-rates-changed/#:~:text=Between%202002%20and%202019%20(I,from%2010%25%20to%205.6%25.

[27] Harvard University (2024). *Admissions Statistics.* https://college.harvard.edu/admissions/admissions-statistics

[28] Harvard University (2024). *Admissions Statistics.* https://college.harvard.edu/admissions/admissions-statistics

[29] Selingo, J. (2020). Who Gets in and Why. A Year inside College Admissions. Scribner

[30] Ivy Wise (2024). *College Admission Statistics.* https://www.ivywise.com/ivywise-knowledgebase/admission-statistics/

[31] Ivy Wise (2024). *College Admission Statistics.* https://www.ivywise.com/ivywise-knowledgebase/admission-statistics/

[32] Statistica (2024). *U.S. colleges whose graduates (All Alumni) earn the most in 2021/22, ranked by starting and mid-career salary.* https://www.statista.com/statistics/244473/top-us-colleges-by-starting-and-mid-career-pay-of-graduates/

[33] Miller, C.C. & Bhatia, A. (2023). *How Big Is the Legacy Boost at Elite Colleges?* The New York Times. https://www.nytimes.com/2023/07/27/upshot/ivy-league-legacy-admissions.html

[34] Morse, R. & Brooks, E. (2023). *How U.S. News Calculated the 2024 Best Colleges Rankings.* US News and World Report. https://www.usnews.com/education/best-colleges/articles/how-us-news-calculated-the-rankings

[35] National Center for Educational Statistics (2022). *Educational Institutions.* https://nces.ed.gov/fastfacts/display.asp?id=1122#:~:text=How%20many%20postsecondary%20educational%20institutions,with%207%2C021%20in%202010%E2%80%9311

[36] Educational Testing Service (2024). *The GRE General Test.* https://www.ets.org/gre/test-takers/general-test/register.html

[37] AAMC (2024). *Taking the MCAT Exam.* Association of American Medical Colleges. https://students-residents.aamc.org/taking-mcat-exam/taking-mcat-exam

[38] LSAC (2024). *The LSAT.* Law School Admission Council. https://www.lsac.org/lsat

[39] Sloan, K. (2022). *ABA votes to end law schools' LSAT requirement, but not until 2025.* Reuters. https://www.reuters.com/legal/legalindustry/aba-votes-end-law-schools-lsat-requirement-not-until-2025-2022-11-18/

[40] Niche (2024). *2024 Best Community Colleges in California.* https://www.niche.com/colleges/search/best-community-colleges/s/california/

[41] California Community Colleges (2024). *Student Enrollment and Demographics.* https://www.cccco.edu/About-Us/Chancellors-Office/Divisions/Digital-Innovation-and-Infrastructure/research-data-analytics/data-snapshot/student-demographics#:~:text=How%20many%20students%20are%20enrolled,is%20closer%20to%201.8%20million

References

[42] Niche (2024). *2024 Best Community Colleges in California.* https://www.niche.com/colleges/search/best-community-colleges/s/california/

[43] Foothill College (2024). *Prospective International Students. Tuition and Fees.* https://foothill.edu/international/prospective/tuition_and_fees.html

[44] Cal State (2024). *Campus Mandatory Fees (2023-24).* https://www.calstate.edu/attend/paying-for-college/csu-costs/tuition-and-fees/campus-mandatory-fees

Cal State (2024). *CSU Tuition.* https://www.calstate.edu/attend/paying-for-college/csu-costs/tuition-and-fees/Pages/basic-tuition-and-fees.aspx

[45] University of California (2024). *Tuition and Cost of Attendance.* https://admission.universityofcalifornia.edu/tuition-financial-aid/tuition-cost-of-attendance/

[46] University of California (2024). *Transfer Admissions Guarantee (TAG).* https://admission.universityofcalifornia.edu/admission-requirements/transfer-requirements/uc-transfer-programs/transfer-admission-guarantee-tag.html

[47] CSU (2023). *Fact Book 2023.* https://www.calstate.edu/csu-system/about-the-csu/facts-about-the-csu/Documents/facts2023.pdf#:~:text=Students%20learn%20from%20world%2D class%20faculty%2C%20gain%20valuable,career%20advising%20to%20ensure%20t hey%20graduate%20job%2Dready

[48] California State University (2024). *Freshman Admission Requirements.* https://www.calstate.edu/apply/freshman/getting_into_the_csu/pages/admissio n-requirements.aspx#hsGradScroll

[49] California State University (2024). *Impacted Undergraduate Majors and Universities, 2024-25.* https://www.calstate.edu/attend/degrees-certificates-credentials/Pages/impacted-degrees.aspx

[50] California State University (2024). *International Student: Admission Requirements.* https://www.calstate.edu/apply/international/getting-into-the-csu/

[51] California State University (2024). *Redirection.* https://www.calstate.edu/apply/redirection

[52]California State University (2024). *Cal State Apply.* https://www.calstate.edu/apply/freshman/Documents/freshman-application-guide-23-24.pdf

[53]University of California (2023). *At a Glance.* https://ucop.edu/institutional-research-academic-planning/_files/uc-facts-at-a-glance.pdf

[54]US News (2024). *Best National University Rankings.* https://www.usnews.com/best-colleges/rankings/national-universities

[55]US News (2024). *Top Public Schools.* https://www.usnews.com/best-colleges/rankings/national-universities/top-public

[56]University of California (2023). *Freshman requirements.* https://admission.universityofcalifornia.edu/admission-requirements/freshman-requirements/

[57]University of California (2024). *University of California application totals for fall 2024 admission on the rise.* https://www.universityofcalifornia.edu/press-room/university-california-application-totals-fall-2024-admission-riseaumentan-el-total-de#:~:text=The%20University%20of%20California%20today,compared%20to%20the%20previous%20year

[58]University of California (2024). *A-G Course List.* https://hs-articulation.ucop.edu/agcourselist

[59]University of California (2024). *A-G Course List.* https://hs-articulation.ucop.edu/agcourselist

[60]University of California (2024). *Preparing Freshman Applicants.* https://admission.universityofcalifornia.edu/counselors/preparing-freshman-students/

[61]University of California (2024). *Freshman Admit Data.* https://admission.universityofcalifornia.edu/campuses-majors/freshman-admit-data.html

[62]University of California (2024). *Subject Requirement (A - G).* https://admission.universityofcalifornia.edu/admission-requirements/freshman-requirements/subject-requirement-a-g.html

References

[63] University of California (2024). *International Applicants. Applying for Admission.* https://admission.universityofcalifornia.edu/admission-requirements/international-applicants/applying-for-admission/

[64] University of California (2024). *Freshman. Additional Information by Country.* https://admission.universityofcalifornia.edu/admission-requirements/international-applicants/applying-for-admission/freshman-requirements-country.html

[65] University of California (2024). *Subject Requirement (A - G).* https://admission.universityofcalifornia.edu/admission-requirements/freshman-requirements/subject-requirement-a-g.html

[66] University of California (2024). *A-G Course List.* https://hs-articulation.ucop.edu/agcourselist

[67] University of California (2024). *International Applicants. Subject Requirement (A-G).* https://admission.universityofcalifornia.edu/admission-requirements/freshman-requirements/subject-requirement-a-g.html

[68] University of California (2024). *How Applicants are Reviewed.* https://admission.universityofcalifornia.edu/how-to-apply/applying-as-a-freshman/how-applications-are-reviewed.html

[69] University of California Berkeley (2023). *First-Year Policy Changes.* https://admissions.berkeley.edu/apply-to-berkeley/freshmen/freshman-policy-changes/

[70] University of California (2024). *Apply Now.* https://admission.universityofcalifornia.edu/apply-now.html#:~:text=UC%20does%20not%20require%20(nor,sure%20to%20check%20your%20email.

[71] University of California (2024). *Nine Campuses. One Application.* https://apply.universityofcalifornia.edu/my-application/login

[72] University of California (2024). *Comprehensive Review.* https://admission.universityofcalifornia.edu/counselors/preparing-freshman-students/comprehensive-review.html

[73] University of California (2024). *Freshman Admissions by Campus and Residency.* https://www.ucop.edu/institutional-research-academic-planning/_files/factsheets/2023/admission-table-1-1.pdf

[74] University of California (2024). *Local Guarantee (ELC).* https://admission.universityofcalifornia.edu/admission-requirements/freshman-requirements/california-residents/local-guarantee-elc.html

[75] University of California. *Statewide Guarantee.* https://admission.universityofcalifornia.edu/admission-requirements/freshman-requirements/california-residents/statewide-guarantee/#:~:text=The%20updated%20Statewide%20Index%20is,campus%2C%20if%20space%20is%20available.

[76] Selingo, J. (2020). Who Gets in and Why. A Year inside College Admissions. Scribner

[77] University of California Los Angeles (2024). *UCLA sees surge in 2024 transfer applications, uptick in first-year California applicants.* https://newsroom.ucla.edu/releases/ucla-applications-for-fall-2024-admission#:~:text=University%20News-,UCLA%20sees%20surge%20in%202024%20transfer%20applications,in%20first%2Dyear%20California%20applicants&text=UCLA%20received%20a%20total%20of,2%25%20rise%20over%20last%20year

[78] University of Michigan (2024). *Selection Process.* https://admissions.umich.edu/apply/first-year-applicants/selection-process

[79] University of California (2024). *Comprehensive Review.* https://admission.universityofcalifornia.edu/counselors/preparing-freshman-students/comprehensive-review.html

[80] Moody, J. (2021). *Universities, Colleges Where Students Are Eager to Enroll.* https://www.usnews.com/education/best-colleges/articles/universities-colleges-where-students-are-eager-to-enroll

[81] Ivy Coach (2024). *Ivy League Admission Statistics for the Class of 2027.* https://www.ivycoach.com/ivy-league-admission-statistics-for-the-class-of-2027/

[82] Laskowski, A. (2024). *Applications for the BU Class of 2028 Are In: Here's What We Know So Far.* https://www.bu.edu/articles/2024/applications-for-bu-class-of-2028/?utm_source=facebook&utm_medium=photo&utm_content=student&utm_campaign=social_main

[83] Stanford University (2024). *First Year Applicants. Regular Decision and Restrictive Early Action.* https://admission.stanford.edu/apply/first-year/decision_process.html

References

[84] Arizona State University (2024). *First-year student college admission requirements.* https://admission.asu.edu/apply/first-year/admission

[85] Steele, E. (2023). *Taking a closer look at Common App Direct Admissions.* https://www.commonapp.org/blog/taking-closer-look-common-app-direct-admissions

[86] CommonApp (2024). *What is account rollover?.* https://appsupport.commonapp.org/applicantsupport/s/article/What-do-I-need-to-know-about-Account-Rollover

[87] CommonApp (2024). *Application guide for first-year students.* https://www.commonapp.org/apply/first-year-students

[88] University of California (2024). *Nine Campuses. One Application.* https://apply.universityofcalifornia.edu/my-application/login

[89] California State University (2024). *Find your Future at the California State University.* https://www.calstate.edu/apply

[90] California State University (2024). *Application Dates and Deadlines.* https://www.calstate.edu/apply/Pages/application-dates-deadlines.aspx

[91] ApplyTexas (2024). *Many Schools. One Application.* https://www.applytexas.org/

[92] State University of New York (2024). *applySUNY.* https://www.suny.edu/applysuny/

[93] Massachusetts Institute of Technology (2024). *MIT Application Portal.* https://apply.mitadmissions.org/portal/apply

[94] Georgetown University (2024). *Georgetown University Application.* https://uapply.georgetown.edu/apply/?sr=634ea7d6-2aab-485c-80bc-4dba7c0d87f8

[95] United States Military Academy West Point (2024). *Information for International Cadets.* https://www.westpoint.edu/admissions/prospective-cadets/international-cadets

[96] United States Naval Academy (2024). *International Candidates.* https://www.usna.edu/Admissions/Apply/International-Candidates.php

[97] Stanford University (2024). *University Communications. Stanford Common Data Set.* https://ucomm.stanford.edu/wp-content/uploads/sites/15/2024/02/stanford-cds-2023_2024_final_v1.pdf

[98] University of California (2024). *Apply Now.* https://admission.universityofcalifornia.edu/apply-now.html#:~:text=UC%20does%20not%20require%20(nor,sure%20to%20check%20your%20email

[99] U.S. Department of Education (2024). *Federal TRIO Programs.* https://www2.ed.gov/about/offices/list/ope/trio/index.html

[100] CommonApp (2020). *Brag Sheet. Student Questionnaire for teacher letter of recommendation.* https://www.commonapp.org/static/71f67faedd72b3cdaf1c28ed85d621cf/FYBragSheetStudentsTeachersCAReady.pdf

[101] Zoom (2024). https://zoom.us/

[102] Initial View (2024). *Tell admissions officers your story.* https://initialview.com/home

[103] Swarthmore College (2024). *Request an Interview. Interviews and Video Responses.* https://www.swarthmore.edu/admissions-aid/request-interview

[104] Apple (2024). https://apps.apple.com/us/app/imovie/id377298193

[105] SlideRoom (2024). https://www.slideroom.com/

[106] GetAcceptd (2024). *The Premier Application and Audition Management Platform.* https://getacceptd.com/

[107] ETS (2024). TOEFL. *Opening doors to a wide and diverse world.* https://www.ets.org/toefl.html

[108] IELTS (2024). *The world's most trusted English test.* https://www.ielts.org

[109] U.S. Department of Homeland Security (2024). *Study in the States. School Search.* https://studyinthestates.dhs.gov/school-search

[110] Harvard College (2024). *What is included in the Harvard supplement?.* https://college.harvard.edu/resources/faq/what-included-harvard-supplement

[111] Harper, S. (2023). *Legacy Admissions At Harvard And Other Elite Institutions Advantage White Applicants, New Evidence Shows.* Forbes. https://www.forbes.com/sites/shaunharper/2023/07/05/legacy-admissions-at-

References

harvard-and-other-elite-institutions-privilege-white-applicants-new-evidence-reveals/?sh=4d6665ea593b

[112] Stanford University (2024). *Admissions considerations for children of alumni or donors.* Stanford Report. https://news.stanford.edu/report/2020/06/26/admissions-considerations-for-children-of-alumni-or-donors/

[113] Miller, H. & Sanchez, O. (2024). *Maryland becomes the third state to completely ban legacy preference in admissions.* The Hechinger Report. https://hechingerreport.org/maryland-to-become-the-third-state-to-completely-ban-legacy-preference-in-admissions/

[114] Hudl (2024). *Change the Way You See the Game.* https://www.hudl.com/

[115] National Collegiate Athletics Association (2024). https://www.ncaa.com/

[116] National Collegiate Athletics Association (2024). *Eligibility Center.* https://web3.ncaa.org/ecwr3/

[117] Williams (2024). *Fast Facts about Williams.* https://communications.williams.edu/media-relations/fast-facts/#:~:text=Approximately%2035%25%20of%20all%20students,and%20a%20large%20intramural%20program

[118] Murphy, D. & Thamel, P. (2024). *NCAA, Power 5 agree to deal that will let schools pay players.* ESPN. https://www.espn.com/college-sports/story/_/id/40206364/ncaa-power-conferences-agree-allow-schools-pay-players

[119] National Association of Collegiate Esports (2024). *Online Directory.* https://members.nacesports.org/AF_MemberDirectory.asp?

[120] National Center for Educational Statistics (2024). *Fast Facts. Endowment.* https://nces.ed.gov/fastfacts/display.asp?id=73

[121] UC Scout (2024). *Course Catalog.* https://www.ucscout.org/courses/

[122] Khan Academy (2024). https://www.khanacademy.org/

[123] Selingo, J. (2020). Who Gets in and Why. A Year inside College Admissions. Scribner

[124] Common Data Set Initiative (2024). https://commondataset.org/

[125]Dartmouth (2024). *Update to Testing Policy.* https://admissions.dartmouth.edu/apply/update-testing-policy

[126]Yale (2024). *Standardized Testing Requirements and & Policies.* https://admissions.yale.edu/standardized-testing

[127]AmeriCorps (2024). *Presidential Recognition for Your Volunteers.* https://presidentialserviceawards.gov/

[128]University of California (2024). *Personal Insight Questions.* https://admission.universityofcalifornia.edu/how-to-apply/applying-as-a-freshman/personal-insight-questions.html

[129]Big Future (2024). *Your Future. Your Way.* https://bigfuture.collegeboard.org/

[130]The Princeton Review (2024). *The Best 389 Colleges.* https://www.princetonreview.com/college-rankings/best-colleges

[131]National Center for Educational Statistics (2024). *College Navigator.* https://nces.ed.gov/collegenavigator/

[132]Fiske, E. (2024). *Fiske Guide to Colleges 2025. 41st Edition*. Sourcebooks (release date: 07/09/2024)

[133]Homeland Security (2024). *Study in the States. School Search.* https://studyinthestates.dhs.gov/school-search

[134]U.S. News (2023). *20 U.S. Colleges That Offer the Most Financial Aid to International Students.* https://www.usnews.com/education/best-colleges/paying-for-college/articles/colleges-that-offer-the-most-financial-aid-to-international-students

[135]U.S. Department of Education (2024). *Net Price Calculator Center.* https://collegecost.ed.gov/net-price

[136]U.S. Department of Education (2024). *Campus Safety and Security.* https://ope.ed.gov/campussafety/#/

[137]USA.gov (2024). *Find Crime Statistics.* https://www.usa.gov/crime-statistics

[138]University of California Davis (2024). *Computer Science. Admission Requirements.* https://cs.ucdavis.edu/graduate/prospective-students/admission-requirements

[139]National Association for College Admissions Counseling (2024). *Support for School Counselors.* https://www.nacacnet.org/advocacy/support-for-school-counselors/

References

[140] National Association for College Admissions Counseling (2024). *Support for School Counselors*. https://www.nacacnet.org/advocacy/support-for-school-counselors/

[141] National Association of College Admission Counseling (2024). *School Counselors Contribute to College Access and Success*. https://nacacnet.org/wp-content/uploads/2022/08/schoolcounselorscontribute.pdf?_ga=2.117295877.2084946729.1711542088-499643385.1711542088&_gac=1.45770710.1711542092.CjwKCAjwh4-wBhB3EiwAeJsppH9ss0J1n9yJ-_mJeUjwvoCPZ-1mijvQe8WUbThzShdyCBPTJlDwCRoCQngQAvD_BwE&_gl=1*8jmhr0*_ga*NDk5NjQzMzg1LjE3MTE1NDIwODg.*_ga_VBBSWPK81X*MTcxMTU0MjA4Ny4xLjEuMTcxMTU0MjMxMS42MC4wLjA

[142] National Association for College Admission Counseling (2024). https://www.nacacnet.org

[143] Independent Educational Consultants Association (2024). *Welcome to IECA*. https://www.iecaonline.com/

[144] ACT Academy (2024). *ACT Learning Resources*. https://www.act.org/content/act/en/products-and-services/learning-resources.html

[145] Independent Educational Consultants Association & Oregon State University Ecampus (2023). *AXS Companion*. https://open.oregonstate.education/axscompanion/

[146] College Board (2024). *SAT Practice and Preparation*. https://satsuite.collegeboard.org/sat/practice-preparation

[147] College Possible (2024). https://collegepossible.org/

[148] College Advising Corp (2024). *Reimagine Prosperity*. https://collegeadvisingcorps.org/

[149] Get Schooled (2024). https://getschooled.com/

[150] Khan Academy (2024). https://www.khanacademy.org/

[151] Revision Learning (2024). *Make your stories come alive!*. https://www.learnrevision.com/

[152] College Essay Guy (2024). *Your home for college admission support*. https://www.collegeessayguy.com/

[153] University of California (2024). *Transfer credit.* https://admission.universityofcalifornia.edu/admission-requirements/transfer-requirements/preparing-to-transfer/transfer-credit.html

[154] University of California (2024). *Transfer credit.* https://admission.universityofcalifornia.edu/admission-requirements/transfer-requirements/preparing-to-transfer/transfer-credit.html

[155] Yale University (2024). *Financial Aid. Estimated Cost of Attendance.* https://finaid.yale.edu/award-letter/financial-aid-terminology/estimated-cost-attendance

[156] University of Southern California (2024). *Cost of Attendance.* https://financialaid.usc.edu/undergraduate-financial-aid/cost-of-attendance/#chapter=overview

[157] University of Southern California (2024). *Cost of Attendance.* https://financialaid.usc.edu/undergraduate-financial-aid/cost-of-attendance/#chapter=overview

[158] University of California (2024). *Tuition and Cost of Attendance.* https://admission.universityofcalifornia.edu/tuition-financial-aid/tuition-cost-of-attendance/

[159] U.S. Department of Education (2024). https://www.ed.gov/

[160] The Hechinger Report (undated). *OfferLetterDECODER.* http://www.myfinancialaidletter.org/

[161] Federal Student Aid (2024). https://studentaid.gov/h/apply-for-aid/fafsa

[162] College Board (2024). CSS Profile. https://cssprofile.collegeboard.org/

[163] Federal Student Aid (2024). *Eligibility for Non-U.S. Citizens.* https://studentaid.gov/understand-aid/eligibility/requirements/non-us-citizens

[164] Federal Student Aid (2024). *Federal Pell Grants.* https://studentaid.gov/understand-aid/types/grants/pell

[165] National Merit Scholarship Corporation (2024). https://www.nationalmerit.org/

[166] Federal Student Aid (2024). Federal Work-Study jobs help students earn money to pay for college or career school. https://studentaid.gov/understand-aid/types/work-study

References

[167] Federal Student Aid (2024). *Direct Subsidized and Direct Unsubsidized Loans.* https://studentaid.gov/understand-aid/types/loans/subsidized-unsubsidized

[168] Federal Student Aid (2024). *Direct PLUS Loans for Parents.* https://studentaid.gov/understand-aid/types/loans/plus/parent

[169] Calculator.net (2024). *Student Loan Projection Calculator.* https://www.calculator.net/student-loan-calculator.html

[170] U.S. Department of Homeland Security (2024). *Study in the States. School Search.* https://studyinthestates.dhs.gov/school-search

[171] U.S. Department of Homeland Security (2024). *Student and Exchange Visitor Program.* https://www.ice.gov/sevis

[172] U.S. Department of State (2024). Online Nonimmigrant Visa Application (DS-160). https://ceac.state.gov/genniv/

Printed in Great Britain
by Amazon

44912898R10165